I Am Here, Why?

I Am Here, Why?

Introspective Stories of Intention

Scott Berger, Marla Berger

Waterside Productions

Cover Design by Marla Berger and Justin Berger

ISBN-13: 978-1-960583-05-5 print edition
ISBN-13: 978-1-960583-06-2 e-book edition

Waterside Productions
2055 Oxford Ave
Cardiff, CA 92007
www.waterside.com

for our family,

*… and for our friends, communities, and all of
our brothers and sisters around the world,*

who continue to inspire and uplift us

CONTENTS

ACKNOWLEDGMENTS

F rom the perspective of extraordinary experiences, and things people attend to: we arrive through the way in which we feel, and think about "being *for* the world, *with* the planet, *from* the whole." We share this perspective, because of the intentional way we feel and think about being *with* one another – *with* families, friends, and communities we've developed meaningful connections; and being *for* one another – *for* individuals, families, and communities who have yet to arrive...

Our most sincere thank you for the thoughtful guidance of Dr. Stephen Hobbs, (our senior programming colleague), who's encouraged and spent endless conversations with us; as to "clarify with consistency," the lines and boxes of our overarching point of view. In addition, Dr. Hobbs has helped us organize, create, and shape our point of view: in view of meaningful perspective; and inspired us to bridge the space, the interrelation and common link between these stories, as to connect them together, for a dynamic balance [and focus] within:

I Am Here, Why?

Our most sincere thank you to everyone who's enlightened us; and has added meaning and perspective to this book: to all the people with whom we've had conversations; and have participated by sharing their thoughts, perspective, and transformational stories along the way: all of which has helped us to build and grow within the **Tree of Life Movement**: "*for* the world, *with* planet, *from* the whole."

* * *

We are grateful to celebrate these stories of intention, (of extraordinary experiences), within the grand journey of life; for our family and friends, our communities, our dear brothers and sisters, and all of the students, around the world, in search of light, love, and gratitude. It is our intention to uplift the *approach, perspective, outcome* to **discover**, **develop**, and **discern** one's truth. And, from the point of view that intention gifts attention: we expand, discern, and clarify the truth of our reality; as it relates to, and exists within self.

As intention gifts attention to <u>stay present</u> and <u>stay found</u>, this connection between intention and attention must start from within… to therefore move fromward and forward; so, the overall connection of self and others begins to mend itself and strengthen for the better. Thus, with a more heightened sense of awareness for both self and others, the relation between the two strengthens and improves.

Within the unifying aspect of intention, we aspire to become more open-minded with empathy for ourselves and everyone around us: thus to see the bigger picture: and, therefore, to view ourselves as being part of (and within) the collective – rather than being apart from (and without) the collective, as separate individuals; in a world that progressively changes, and adapts day by day…

* * *

Lastly, we acknowledge the existential philosophy of Ubuntu, which demonstrates and encourages a substantial point of view:

"I am because we are ..." for a world of clarity, confidence, and *Oneness.* The key aspect (or core element) which Ubuntu attends to and shares from is the *"belief in a universal bond of sharing that connects all humanity."*

From the perspective of Ubuntu, as it relates to and connects with intention and attention, we discover, develop, and discern more awareness: to create stronger, more sustainable, (in)tentional boundaries, connections, and experiences with our self, with people we meet, and with our family, friends, and communities; and, ultimately, the world.

This unified effort to *shine light* from one moment: one experience, one connection, and one boundary to another ... is, therefore, to amplify the overall light of our inner self; and discern the voice from which we communicate.

OUR INTENTIONAL BLESSING FOR YOU

———

Close your eyes and take a deep breath through your nose so you can ground yourself. First and foremost, may you receive blessings of health, light, love, courage and strength to continue to fill up your beautiful hearts and souls with unconditional love, which will allow you to fully heal. This will allow you to continue to help so many more brothers and sisters heal, which will unify all mankind, so we may all see heaven on earth as it is here now and our true purpose in life to be our authentic selves.

OUR PURPOSE AND MISSION

Our purpose is to shift consciousness and awaken
people to the powers within themselves; to transform
personal circumstances; and to create positive change
in world; ultimately, connecting all humanity as one.

* * *

Our mission is to unify the collective of humanity
through a global spiritual awakening, ignited by
the realization of the power held by intention.

INTROSPECTIVE STORIES OF
INTENTION

———

*I*Am Here, Why? shares (in)tentional, (in)timate, and (in)trospective stories about meaningful connections from the Tree of Life Movement. These introspective stories of intention, individually, and as they are woven together explore the question, "I Am Here, Why?". These stories, as they reflect meaningful connections with self, with people they've just met, and with family, friends, and communities, demonstrate dynamic shifts of negative to positive connections and experiences, and demonstrate physical-and-emotional transformations of healing.

With the mission and purpose of connecting all humanity as one, the *unifying* aspect of positive intention, people are connecting with and reflecting on their past experiences, connections, and boundaries; as to move onward, upward, and forward; as a way to attend and interact with the present moment.

With the *unifying* aspect of intention – as intention gifts attention to **stay present**, **stay found**, and **shine light**, (this awareness which arrives from a more heartfelt connection with self and others) – people are inspired to gift Tree of Life Intention Sticks to their family, friends, and communities; as to create more positive energy to ripple through their boundaries, connections, and experiences; and, by extension, the world.

As each person gifts or receives an Intention Stick, and the blessings of Intention, this encourages us to attend to our connections and experiences: for both our self, and the people in our lives. The Tree of Life Movement founded, and created the Tree of Life Intention Stick, which is, in its practical application, an intention-based technology: applied by the use of this spiritual tool: which is a constant and physical reminder as one selects, shares, and wears their intentions over their heart.

Every individual who receives, wears, and applies their Tree of Life Intention Stick *discovers*, *develops*, and *discerns* their own truth and reality; from which these stories of intention arise. Because these stories are transformational, the messages which we connect to and with, as we read these experiences, helps us to improve, focus, and strengthen; helps us (the collective *us*) to better ourselves within the collective: as human beings.

* * *

*"There are two ways to live your life. One is
as though nothing is a miracle. The other is
as though everything is a miracle."*
[Albert Einstein]

START WITH A CELEBRATION
– 1 –

Marla:

A MIRACLE OCCURS after an exceptionally meaningful experience and conversation with Dr. Wayne Johnson; a brilliant inventor and scientist who connects with us to consider a new technology, and application for the Tree of Life Movement.

Scott and I receive an endearing, heartfelt, request, a phone call from Dr. Johnson, the following day... "My wife Deb has been battling Multiple Sclerosis (MS) for thirteen years," Dr. Johnson shares. "Deb is very fond of jewelry. I'm at my wits' end as to finding Deb a Christmas gift: is it possible to create a rose gold Intention Stick?"

With a ten-day timeframe leading up to Christmas, there are a few challenges we need to consider... because the Intention Stick is still a prototype; the twenty-two words of intention have not been scaled out; and the cost of casting the piece in rose gold is not determined... yet, we have trust, and complete faith.

"Of course! We can design this gift for Deb."

On Christmas Eve, Dr. Johnson and his wife, Deb, arrive at our office; where Dr. Johnson gifts, and places the Intention Stick over Deb's heart...

"My goodness! I feel the warmth around my neck," Deb exclaims.

"Wayne totally surprised me with this gift," Deb emphasizes. "Scott shared with me the guiding aspect of the Intention Stick. I remember thinking, 'this is beautiful!' as Wayne placed this over my heart. I could feel the warmth, and it took my breath away... I was overcome with emotion and began to cry."

"I couldn't imagine this experience, which had such a transformational effect on me, without experiencing it for myself; and is exactly what continues to happen... as I wear the Intention Stick, it guides and encourages me to continue forward; to face the hardships in adverse times that confront me along the way."

* * *

Two years later, in 2018, we gift Dr. Johnson an Intention Stick; from which Dr. Johnson shares his interactions, and transformational story, when we speak with him and Deb, in June of 2020...

"I'm bulletproof, I'm mindful reasoning, I focus on the present," Dr. Johnson shares. "I spin on my heels when something's a problem. I'm strictly open to trusting my personal relationships. And I've grown an incredible volume of work with people. All of which has happened because of the Intention Stick," Dr. Johnson affirms.

There are no coincidences Dr. Johnson and Deb arrived in our life during the prototype stage of the Intention Stick. We are guided to one another – to each beautiful soul – and we believe experiences and lessons show up for a reason. Our point of view is to remain open, and say "yes" to the universe.

THE INSPIRATION FOR THE
INTENTION STICK
− 2 −

Scott:

The Tree of Life is an ancient, universal symbol, established as a theme in many religious and spiritual traditions; and represents the source of divine wisdom. Because of my profound interest in, and respect for the Tree of Life, this inspired me to design a Tree of Life pendant: with the symbol engraved on the front, and our four children's names engraved on the back; for Marla, on our twenty-one-year anniversary: December 22, 2011.

"Two souls come together for a divine reason, and purpose," Marla emphasizes, as she opens the jewelry box, and sees the pendant inside. "This is it!"

* * *

It's September 2016: we are asked to design a jewelry collection for the Pope's charity, which includes all the world's flags to support refugee children around the world. One of the jewelry pieces which we designed for this collection is a Tree of Life pendant: with the charity's globe engraved on one side; and, on the other side, is the symbol of the Tree of Life.

Gabriel, (who's the Pope's right-hand man), visits one of the schools in Arizona, associated with the the Pope's charity. In addition, a Cardinal from Ethiopia is accompanying Gabriel. Because they are in Arizona, both of them visit our gallery, which presents us with an incredible opportunity to gift Gabriel with the Tree of Life pendant; as well as a Tree of Life charm bracelet to gift to Gabriel's wife.

In the midst of this incredibly meaningful conversation with Gabriel and the Cardinal, I share "we are all these drops of beautiful light; and, we're going to push through all of the darkness in the world; because we are all one."

"Yes, I agree with you my son … and you must spread that light and love throughout the world," the Cardinal affirms; and acknowledges.

* * *

Some time after … I receive an inspiring vision in my morning meditation; an image of a tube appears. Then, one month later, in a similar meditation, this image of the tube appears, again: and this time, with the Tree of Life symbol. I share this connection of seeing the Tree of Life symbol, wrapped around the tube, with Marla. As I begin to understand more clearly, what I've been experiencing in this and the previous meditation, Marla and I close our eyes to meditate …

Within our own individual meditations, we both receive messages and words. The messages and words we receive, are the twenty-two words of intention:

Oneness	Health
Believe	Consciousness
Faith	Inspire
Gratitude	Laugh/Joy
Mindful	Courage
Be/Let It Be	Happiness
Love	Spiritual
Light	Trust
Blessed	Knowledge
Peace	Success
Kindness	Compassion

Marla and I created the Tree of Life Intention Stick, because we believe, from our hearts, there is a bigger purpose to all of this; how this will be meaningful for our family and friends, our communities, and everyone in the world: to inspire, uplift, and help one another; to find meaning and purpose in life; to expand our hearts, our minds, and our points of view; and to focus on positive intention, for positive attention ...

Twenty-Two Words of
Intention
– 3 –

There is a concept called Tikkun, which means *"repair."* As Tikkun relates to self, as we think, perceive, and interact (in relation to self, and everyone around us), this encourages us to repair our inner self: by creating an inner focus of awareness.

We apply this concept of Tikkun to focus, improve, and strengthen our relation to self ... to focus, improve, and strengthen our perception from which we think, perceive, and interact: in relation to, and connection with things (the varying degrees and aspects); people (their values and interests); the world (the cultures and dynamics); and the world within (the reality and thoughts from which we contemplate).

The extending aspect of Tikkun, is to repair the world (Olam); and, by extension, to repair the connection which bridges everyone, and everything, together. The concept of Tikkun Olam encourages us to focus, improve, and strengthen our connection – from self to others – for a substantial purpose: *"in pursuit of social justice,"* for the world ...

* * *

Our attention arrives from our intention: *what* we attend to, (*what* we're doing), *where* our focus is, *who* we're with … and, is based on how we perceive our self. So, as we discern our truth, is there something within us, upon which we can focus, improve, and strengthen to create the substantial awareness to be more vigilant of self (of our thoughts, emotions, behavior-patterns, actions, reactions, interactions, and the like): of others: and of the world around us?

Because intention creates, grows, and strengthens awareness based on the perspective – the angle and point of view – which they're applied, considered, and contemplated, our connections to *what* we attend to (*what* we're doing), *who* we're with, *where* we're going, and *where* our focus is, all intensify from a strengthened awareness, a stronger perspective, and connection with self. Thus, from a stronger sense of awareness, as individuals and as individuals part of a collective, this encourages us to focus, improve, and strengthen – thus repair – the overall connection within self.

* * *

In view of Kabbalah, each intention has different interpretations, and can be applied in different ways. This aspect of interpretations, is also known as seventy-two names of God; and, as seventy-two interpretations … from which we add the premise that each intention is not limited to its one defining word. Yet each intention connects with either one aspect, or many different aspects, of how we perceive our intentions: this is to say, how we identify with our self, in relation to one aspect or another, in relation to one person, or everyone around us: is all part of the interpretation of the intentions we select, share, and wear; thus, how we apply each intention in relation to the present moment...

The Intention of *Faith* encompasses the aspect of hope. This is to say, hope is a softer, more subtle, aspect of the Intention of *Faith* – which has a stronger connotation and clearer aim. The Intention of *Success* represents many different aspects in life: such as creating *success* within a relationship; *success* for health; *success* in finance; or *success* in relation to another intention... the Intention of *Success* in relation to the Intention of *Faith*; having *success* in one's *faith*, and vice-versa: having *faith* in *success*.

This [establishing a] relation between intentions, and creating a formula of linking intentions together, focuses, improves, and strengthens the overall connection to your inner self, to others, and to your inner purpose with an *Intention Gifts Attention* point of view. The Intention of *Be, Let It Be*, (an intention to surrender one's attachment to the outcome within any circumstance), can be linked with the Intention of *Faith*, (an intention to reinforce certainty and belief in the best possible outcome).

As you select your intentions for your Intention Stick, be exceptionally honest with yourself. This is to say: which intention will help you, whether it's for something significant, and purposeful in your life – or something more subtle?; which intention, or intentions, will help encourage, and guide you to be of more service to others, and your self?

In addition, it is important to be thoughtful of our intentions, and of how many intentions we select, share, and wear inside the Intention Stick. It has been brought to our attention: too many intentions can be spiritually and energetically heavy. To emphasize this point of view; that *too many intentions can be spiritually and energetically heavy*: our friend expresses to Marla and I that he is experiencing immense discomfort in his neck; we discover there are eight intentions inside his Intention Stick; so we suggest changing his intentions to only one, two, or (at most) three; the pain in his neck quickly alleviates ... and so, we recommend, either one, two, or three intentions at a time.

Based on each circumstance, we may be inspired to change an intention; as to move forward, through any moment, gracefully: with the least amount of pain and suffering. Therefore, intentions can be changed daily, monthly, or once a year. As you wear this spiritual tool close to your heart, it is a constant and physical reminder of your intentions: *what, who, or where* you are impelled towards; or *what* you impel yourself towards; as you discern your truth, in pursuit of your purpose.

SHIFTING CONSCIOUSNESS AT WINDSOR CASTLE

– 4 –

"Dear Scott and Marla ... It is my honour to invite
the two of you to participate in a private Windsor
Workshop for Leaders inside Windsor Castle."

Marla:

This incredible invitation to participate in the Windsor Workshop, October of 2016, describes a residential retreat at St George's House, inside Windsor Castle. This is the exact location where, in the 600-year-old Vicars' Hall, William Shakespeare performed his play *The Merry Wives of Windsor* in front of Queen Elizabeth I.

The theme (and purpose) of this four-day event is "to engage with the challenges involved in shifting consciousness, as visionaries and world leaders, in ways that make it natural for us to come up with outcomes that we previously thought impossible!" And the invitation is signed by: "Pete Ashby, Leadership Director, St George's House, Windsor Castle." We confirm the details and feel truly blessed to participate and be a part of this incredible opportunity.

* * *

It's Sunday: when we arrive at Windsor Castle. The first evening in St George's House, we are seated at the head of a table ... set for twenty-six people! Among the participants are physicians, professors, healers, musicians, and corporate executives from the U.K., U.S., and Canada.

Before dinner, Scott is asked to do blessings and prayers for the group.

Scott:

"Just be in the now ... be present," I think to myself. First, I say the blessings for both the wine and bread; and then, everyone holds hands. "These next four days should be filled with light, love, and a way for us to figure out how we're going to help heal the world," I affirm. "When we do something meaningful, it should come from within ... – from our heart." The following days, we meet for roundtable sessions in Vicars' Hall; and our conversations hint at themes surrounding the Tree of Life.

The Jewish celebration of Simchat Torah occurs during our visit and workshop at the Castle. Simchat Torah is a holiday that celebrates the end of the yearly Torah readings with singing, dancing, and drinking. Since Marla and I are the only people in the group who celebrate the Jewish holiday, I express the significance of observing this holiday to everyone in St George's Tea Room.

Prior to this evening, I imagine that this celebration has never taken place inside the Castle. The entire group, 26 people including Charlotte, who is the 3rd generation assistant to the Queen, is in St George's Tea Room. As per the holiday tradition, it is customary, after reading each prayer (from the five books of Moses), to celebrate with a drink.

"I'm in!"; each person in the group responds.

In very Orthodox Jewish communities, there are different degrees of how to celebrate Simchat Torah; and the Jewish community whom I study with... the Rabbi performs a traditional somersault – as a symbolic gesture to bring in the new year. So, as per the Rabbi's tradition, I walk into the middle of the Tea Room, and perform a somersault.

The CFO (of all the embassies) steps forward and, also, performs a somersault. Then, another person steps forward to somersault. This continues until everyone in the room, in this symbolic gesture, performs a somersault to bring in the new year! The celebration continues – as we form a circle, dance (the hora), and sing in the middle of St George's Tea Room.

Charlotte is standing at the doorway, smiling, and watching us celebrate. After the celebration, Charlotte leads us through a private tour of St George's Chapel, (located next to St George's House), where many of the kings and queens are traditionally married. Everyone is immersed in conversation about what we can do to bring the world together, how we can help unify humanity, and about the Tree of Life.

"I'm going to take you to where we do not take the public," Charlotte says; and walks us over to a set of beautifully arched, double red doors... which feature gold imagery on each side of the door. Nearly eight hundred years prior to us arriving at the Castle, these doors were built as the Queen's private entrance from the Castle to the Cathedral. Charlotte directs our view to the design and imagery: "Do you know what this symbol is?" Charlotte asks; and says... "It's the Tree of Life!"

This is an astonishing moment. The surprise of this, all at once, takes the breath away from the entire group. Marla and I look at each other with amazement, and think: "We understand. We get the message!" This moment is a meaningful affirmation

and validation for our purpose with the Tree of Life symbol and
the spiritual connection we all have as a group.

* * *

Richard and Lisa Seppala, our dear friends, and participants in
the retreat, share with Marla and I: "There is so much energy,
and connection, with a group of people who, previously, we've
never met before. And then, to wrap up this private tour with
the symbolic doors of the Tree of Life … this is one of the most
defining moments of what the Tree of Life is, because it connects
so many dots … the story is so powerful; and, in our experience,
this is the defining moment of holy shift: this is for real!"

A Vision for the Tree of Life Movement (An Encouraging Point of View)

– 5 –

Marla:

After the tour in St George's Chapel, we gather at the oldest home on the Castle grounds for a reception. Scott and I arrive at 11:11 PM – the spiritual number that symbolizes the construct of angels surrounding you; affirming, and validating that you're in alignment, and are on the right path.

Pete Ashby reports directly to the royal family, and informs them about the meetings and retreats. Pete is an intuitive and spiritual person, and is a visionary for world leaders; and has been inviting groups of leaders and people, for retreats and gatherings, to the Castle since the 1970's.

"I'd love to take you both aside, and share something with you," Pete says to Scott and I. And, in a serious yet light tone, Pete continues: "When I saw you both arrive on Sunday, and get out of the car, you were surrounded by this beautiful bubble of white light. Last night, I had a vision of your tree, and your tree encompassed the entire world. And underneath your tree, I saw hundreds of thousands of these beautiful white tents, representing every person, every cause, every religion, everyone. It's not a Tree of Life Foundation you've started; it's a Tree of Life Movement. It's much bigger than you possibly could have ever dreamt or imagined."

Scott and I have never thought of the Tree of Life Foundation in this magnitude. We believe when you follow your heart, *you're in alignment, and are on the right path*; thus you're being guided. And there is a strong sense this in our hearts … this is such a life-changing moment for Scott and I to hear this profound, and incredibly powerful message.

Following our conversation with Pete … it's our last day at the Castle. We are back in Vicars' Hall, and the entire group is immersed in a conversation about shifting consciousness. Because of the message Pete shared with Scott and I, Pete emphasizes to everyone: "I think Marla has something to share with the group."

Scott has been exceptionally patient to share the story of Tree of Life Movement, the Intention Stick, and the collection we created for the Pope's foundation to support refugee children, with the group … so, "I think I'd better let Scott speak."

Scott describes the Tree of Life as unifying; it's not about religion, gender, or politics. The Tree of Life is about the right intention: "The spiritual meaning of the Tree of Life is an extension, and expansion of our souls. It's a spiritual symbol and not just a religious symbol. It's about the evolution of consciousness, and about being better than who we were yesterday," Scott says; and continues:

"We're here to learn and grow and expand. But we're also here to help another soul. And what we think about, is what we bring about. Based on the laws of attraction. What goes up, comes down. What we put out from our hearts, comes back to our hearts. If we act and react with kindness, love, gratitude, happiness, joy, and compassion, these positive intentions grow and expand. However, if we react and act with worry, fear, stress and anxiety, these negative intentions grow and expand; and this realization – that we have the ability to shift our consciousness – is the guiding force which led us to create the Intention Stick."

We originally started a Tree of Life Foundation. And, when Pete shares his vision with Scott and I – the Tree of Life Movement encompassing every person, every religion, every cause – it resonates with us to such a degree, that this is the vision we share with the group … the excitement from everyone is so encouraging, and enthusiastic that Scott and I promise to gift an Intention Stick to every participant in the group.

When we arrive in Arizona, contemplating our experiences, and journey at Windsor Castle, our dear friends, Richard and Lisa, continue to inspire us to launch the Tree of Life Movement and the Intention Stick. Because Scott and I think everything has to be perfect, and should be perfect, Richard and Lisa encourage us to move forward with their help, and kind and thoughtful words: "good is good enough."

THE MAGIC OF SPEAKING YOUR TRUTH

– 6 –

Liz Meza

Liz describes herself as daughter, sister, mother, nonni,
and friend. I try to see the beautiful magic exuded
by every human being I meet. We all
carry a little magic within us.

I've been carrying this lump-size golf ball in my throat ever since my mom's passing. I've seen doctors and specialists. I've had MRI scans of my throat; and all of these tests have come back negative. Yet, I can't seem to get rid of this pain in my throat. This pain has weighed so heavy – it's in my back, it's in my shoulders, it's in my brain – I just can't take it anymore...

"Are you okay?" Scott and Marla ask, when I meet them at their office. They're truly open to my response... "I'm not okay." They're sensing what I'm feeling and have been feeling for twenty years.

Scott and Marla welcome and invite me to be open and honest; to express my true self. From this conversation, and interaction, I feel myself begin to release this pain, as we hold hands to do blessing for my Intention Stick ... I choose one word to place inside. Scott places the Intention Stick around my neck, and I burst out crying. I can feel the pain in my throat go away! The lump just suddenly disappears ... as the color rushes back into my face, and rushes back into my world.

"You've been carrying your emotions in your throat. You've been holding everything in, and haven't been able to express your truth," Marla says; and "that's why the lump left."

"You were like this flower that bloomed in front of us," Scott says.

That evening, I write Scott and Marla a letter which I will paraphrase:

I'm sitting here, writing you this letter, sharing with you how for months and months I've been praying and asking for God's help, to find those who have compassion and love in their hearts, to help overcome all the negativity and hatred in this world. I'm sitting here, crying tears of joy, for the answered prayers. The intention that I chose was Be Let It Be, to make sure everything is perfect just as it is, and let go of the things that we cannot control.

I have not had this throat pain since that day, several years ago, when Scott and Marla gifted me with an Intention Stick. *Gratitude* is one of the words I have carried in my Intention Stick ever since that day – this word has kept me grounded.

Marla shares with me that once I get on the momentum of gratitude, I won't be able to stop. This has turned out to be true. I write a gratitude list every day, and I stop at twenty things that I am grateful for; and when you let go, you are able to let other things in. Once there is a shift, once you're open and let the fearful and negative thoughts go, and thus surrender, this allows for the courageous and positive thoughts to come in.

So many things have happened since I received my Intention Stick. I don't know what my comfort zone is anymore; because I've had a lot of boundaries, and now, they're gone. Life has changed dramatically for me. I'm engaged to a wonderful man, a beautiful soul, who is on the same journey with me. He has a son, and his son wears the Intention Stick every day. It's amazing; how one person changing can have a ripple effect on everyone around us …

TRUST TRANSCENDS
EVERYTHING
– 7 –

Andrew Bloom

Andrew is a self-made philanthropist and life coach who came from humble beginnings on the streets of Los Angeles to being one of the top residential Realtors in the world, having sold over $1 billion in residential real estate.

After spending twenty years with an organization whom I respect, trust, and care about, I feel the need to seek other opportunities. So, I sit down with Scott and Marla, who I've known for more than two decades, and share that I'm inspired to make a change; and I seek their advice on making it…

Because I need a tool: a North Star for guidance; to give me faith and the confidence to make this decision, without regret, they gift me a Tree of Life Intention Stick: with the Intention of *Trust* in it. When they place the Intention Stick around my neck, having this Intention of *Trust* in there allows me to stop thinking with my head, to lead with my heart and soul, and just let God and the universe lead me in the direction I need to go.

Letting go of fear, uncertainty, or doubt is one of the greatest gifts that the Intentions Stick gifts to us! … the results are exponentially greater and faster than anything I could ever imagine it would be …

There is an immediate recognition by me; that I am doing the right thing, at the right time, with the right people. Everything I touch, works out, and everything I desire, comes true. I've never taken the Intention Stick off since I received it, and I wear it for a lot of different purposes other than career – such as health, spirituality, and relationships. There are so many ways in which the Intention Stick works, and I'm experiencing it across so many different parts of my life. I've kept the same word in there for more than three years – for me, *Trust* transcends everything.

Because I'm inspired to gift fifty Intention Sticks to my team of realtors, I invite Scott and Marla, so they can share their story and message. Scott and Marla ask everyone to form a circle, and for the entire team to hold hands for an intentional blessing and ceremony. As everyone chooses their words for their Intention Stick, I can feel the room light up with energy; and it literally makes my knees buckle – to the extent that I almost fall over.

My business has grown exponentially, and I believe that one of the reasons is because I embrace the Intention Stick as a way of bringing culture, strength, and courage into my real estate team that's part of a global community. Introducing the Intention Stick to my team has brought us together; and creates a culture within our team where there's just a common denominator that's much deeper, and richer than anything I could ever imagine.

In a place of business, you can't really bring in religion. Yet the Intention Stick is about faith and hope, about sharing and generosity and love, and so many things that translate across any language or culture. This allows me to be a leader in my organization, and to bring compassion, understanding, and hope to everybody on my team. When the people around you connect with your soul, and know that you're invested, I think the working relationship becomes more meaningful. And, what we do collectively, then becomes more successful.

It's significant to see the overall impact that the Intention Stick has brought into my business's expansion, and overall upward-trajectory. We've tracked this. And my business has grown nearly 500% in less than four years. My spiritual growth and my own personal faith have grown proportionately to my business's growth. In fact, I feel that my spiritual and personal faith have probably been greater than the economic growth that we are experiencing. My faith, and trust in what I'm doing in my life, has grown beyond measure.

I've shared the Intention Stick with hundreds of people and have seen the power of the Intention Stick work, immediately, without fail. It's universal, regardless of age, gender, or national origin. I will forever be grateful for the light and energy received from the Tree of Life Intention Stick, and I'm a different person from when I received it. It's a grace to wear this, and it's a grace to be able to listen to other people and gift them positivity and growth.

I am blessed to be able to use the power of the Intention Stick to better who I am, and to help better the people around me. I see the Intention Stick healing people and think that personal growth is all part of healing. Scott and Marla have created a road map for anyone who wants to be the best version of themselves. God chooses messengers for a reason; different messengers throughout history have delivered different messages in different ways. With the Intention Stick, it just so happens that you're carrying this gift and message around with you; and are wearing it right next to your heart.

LOVE ENCOURAGES
MORE LOVE
– 8 –

Sandy and Mark Yozipovic

Mark & Sandy are Senior National Sales Directors with Primerica since 1988, and for over 20 years they†1st have been health advocates for integrative/ naturopathic medicine. For more than a decade they have been involved with Women World Changers, an organization dedicated to the safety and shelter for trafficked women & children.

We are fascinated by Scott and Marla's experience, and connections from Windsor Castle; they were guided to the doorway of St George's Chapel, the image of the Tree of Life symbol ... and, to developing and creating the Tree of Life Intention Stick. All of which seems like a *God-bump* moment. Scott and Marla share that one of the aspects of the Intention Stick encourages and strengthens our connection with God. This connects with us, because of its essence to be neutral and participate in any aspect of life; and the aspects we're interested in, as God inspires within us.

* * *

We have a friend who has been struggling with cancer, and we're inspired to gift an Intention Stick to him … an eight-pound tumor has just been removed from his lungs; and he's at the lowest point of his life, both mentally and physically. We share the story of the Intention Stick – the inspiration for why, and how Scott and Marla created it – and he's blown away. After he selects his intentions, and places them inside, he immediately puts the Intention Stick around his neck; and transforms into a more understanding and peaceful soul as he wears his Intention Stick. From the minute he places it on, his energy changes. He softens into, and becomes a more grateful person; and never takes his Intention Stick off during the next four years that he continues to live.

* * *

Another similar experience: we decide to visit our friend Scott, who has throat cancer, and his wife Lori at their home in Canada; after being informed, "Scott doesn't have long to live." Scott is a full-blown atheist, who holds a lot of anger towards the circumstances of his life. Scott has always been a happy-go-lucky guy; but now, it seems, as if he has a lot of turmoil spreading inside. We bring an Intention Stick for him, and are struggling with how to present the Intention Stick – and whether or not we should even try …

When we arrive at their home in Canada, Scott is waiting for us on their porch, and appears to be excited. We gently bring up the subject about our friends who created the Tree of Life Intention Stick, and show Scott the Intention Stick and how to place the intentions inside. So Scott can get healthy, we share, "you will need to believe in something greater than yourself; something, or someone to believe in, such as God.

"I believe," Scott affirms; without us saying anything more, he chooses his words and places them into his Intention Stick. From this moment forward, his life shifts to a completely different trajectory: he surrenders to his emotions, and shifts his mindset with more enthusiasm.

This letter, which we sent to Scott and Marla, is about our friend, Scott:

Hey guys, just wanted you to know everyone we talked to is blown away with the story of you and the journey of these Intention Sticks. We have seen the toughest nuts break wide open. This is a story about a friend, a former atheist, a hopeless and bitter friend, that let the enemy push him down so far, he had given up the will to live after losing his job, being cheated out of hundreds of thousands of dollars by his own brother, and being diagnosed with cancer, all in less than a year. He has hope after our visit and has agreed to come to Arizona to start treatment for a second chance in life. He has refused all hope to this point. It was your story that changed him. After hearing us tell your story he grabbed his necklace and said out loud, I'm a believer. That was without prayer, guys. That was just your story. This movement will truly change lives and change the world.

When Scott and Lori stay with us in Arizona, as he undergoes cancer treatment, we see the transformation of God working within his life. He's calmer, and more peaceful. His family establishes a GoFundMe page that raises thousands of dollars for his treatment, and Scott is blown away by this; because he never knew so many people cared about him … this realization brings him to tears.

We've learned, from these experiences, as you wear an Intention Stick, this gifts you a feeling of peace. And it helps you to take inventory of your blessings. We believe that gifting an Intention Stick to someone is a symbol of how much they are loved. The Intention Stick is a powerful tool that can act as a *shift-change* when life becomes chaotic or troubling; and wearing this helps keep you stay centered.

The energy of the Intention Stick, and of your journey, as you wear one, begins the minute you select the words of intention and place them inside. Everyone says that two or three words jump out at them; and choosing these words and placing them inside their Intention Stick, symbolizes the start of their journey.

We believe there will be a time when billions of people will be inspired and compelled to wear, and gift Intention Sticks to one another. And, just like finance, with compound interest, this will happen exponentially, over time; because love encourages more love: from which goodness arrives.

Every Day Feels Like a Gift
– 9 –

Lori McGillivary

*Lori is the owner of personal power, purveyor of
mindful peace, relentlessly defining
confidence in a way that is authentic to me.*

M y husband, Scott, was diagnosed with throat cancer in
April 2016:

We learn a few weeks later that it has metastasized to his
lungs, giving him a terminal stage 4 cancer diagnosis. The doctors inform us that Scott has only three to five months to live.
Scott is very pragmatic, and accepts the facts as his fate – this is
his mindset. When Scott begins treatment, he becomes quite ill
and exceptionally weak from the radiation that he doesn't make
it all the way through the treatments:

By the time Mark and Sandy, Scott's friends, visit us in
August, they are really coming to say "goodbye." They bring an
Intention Stick, and want to spend time with Scott, and talk about
faith and belief – about things greater than us. When Mark and
Sandy gift the Intention Stick to Scott, he is so enthralled with the
story, and so impressed with how passionately they are speaking
about it, that he can't help but to jump on board. This gifts hope

to Scott, and something greater than himself to contemplate, and focus on. Then, everything just takes off, and unfolds from here. Sandy and Mark invite us to stay in their home in Arizona, so Scott can begin his cancer treatment at Envita. Their support gives Scott more hope.

While we're in Arizona, we get together with Scott and Marla for dinner, at Mark and Sandy's favorite restaurant; and, in this meaningful interaction, Scott shares that my Scott is surrounded by love, has purpose, and will continue his journey no matter how difficult it becomes; because it's the way in which the Universe, the Source, or God predetermined it to be... my husband is so moved that he breaks down in tears, right there, at the dinner table. To have someone whom he has never met before believe in him is astounding to my husband – and extremely empowering for him to hear.

For me, I have to accept that it's not my journey, it's Scott's journey, and I'm the co-pilot. I'm along to facilitate whichever direction he wants to go. I have to give up control and power, because sometimes we're swimming upstream, and it's just easier to lift your feet and go with the current.

I place my own intentions and mindset into my Intention Stick, and make them powerful. When I'm feeling disconnected, or am not engaging in the way I normally would, I change my mindset by changing out the words in my Intention Stick. This allows me to focus on the kind of intentions I need to place into the universe.

For Scott, it's the Intention of *Health* – this is the big intention I place in there. I also have the Intention of *Be, Let It Be* in there; which is one of my favorites. Every single one of the twenty-two words is applicable to something that Scott and I are going through. Having those words around our necks daily is a powerful reminder to bring us back, every time, to the intentions we set.

Our Intention Sticks are a catalyst for us in maintaining our belief and hope. For Scott, especially, being loved and being seen – is extremely powerful for him, and he starts to really understand how big he is in this world. We both have to learn how to accept the love, the help, and the outpouring that comes our way; because this feels overwhelming, we don't know how to handle this attention.

After his treatments in Arizona, I can tell he's feeling better. His personality starts to come back. And, subsequently, we have a Christmas which has never been promised to us; because the original diagnosis indicates Scott will not make it to Christmas time. He isn't giving up after this; Scott develops more of a long-term view, and the fight returns in him. We also have a great summer, as if it's the best-worst-summer ever. We surround ourselves with the friends who want to see him. Every day feels like a gift. We make the most of every minute we have together. There is a tragic beauty in this; because every minute, we are present in the moment.

Scott's held so much anger from all sorts of challenges, and experiences which have happened; and then he begins to feel free enough to just let everything go. A friend shares with us, "It's like we are a vial – and it is only so big. It holds only so much; and if we don't empty out the vial continuously, to get rid of all the anger and resentments, it will overflow and spill into our life."

At the end of his own life, Scott understands this; and, as a result, he is able to have the most meaningful, and honest relationships and experiences ever. Scott lives eighteen more months after that original cancer diagnosis, and he dies peacefully.

I'm so grateful for every single one of these days that we were blessed to share together, above and beyond those five months that had been predicted for him. His life was cut short, but out of it we gained so many valuable life lessons. We learned the more you give, the more you receive. And we learned that there's very little we can't overcome, if it was meant to be.

A challenge is just that: a challenge. Overcoming is about mindset, and knowing that your mindset can be changed. It's a matter of perspective, of finding serenity, and it's about channeling our intention and giving it power.

I think that gets you through anything. It's something I'm still learning: to give freely and expect nothing in return. Mark and Sandy brought the Intention Stick into our lives at the perfect time, and I'm forever grateful. I'm thrilled at the thought that my story might inspire at least one person reading this: to feel hope, and think, "Okay, I can do this. I can get through this. I will be okay."

(In Loving Memory of Scott McGillivary)

HOLY SHIFT!
– 10 –

Lisa and Richard Sepalla

*Lisa is a wife, mother of four, dentist DMD, and
practice owner, leader, visionary, philanthropist,
spiritual and fun-loving; and Richard is known
as the ROI guy, a husband first and father of
four ... world leader, visionary and entrepreneur,
and multi-bestselling author and Philanthropist.*

Lisa and Richard:

Over four years ago, we meet Scott and Marla, for the first
time, at Windsor Castle. The time we spend with Scott and
Marla, and the leadership group, at "The Windsor Workshop for
Leaders" is where our incredible journey and experience with the
Tree of Life begins ...

Lisa:

Because we're going to have meetings about how we can help
save our business, and help other people save their businesses, I
perceive this as a business trip.

When I walk into that room the first night, I discover that
this is a spiritual group. And I'm not the kind of person who can

discuss spiritual topics with other people; so, I feel uncomfortable. Yet, the people I meet at this retreat are really kind, and open-hearted; such that, you can speak your truth and be honest with everyone.

Before Richard and I meet Scott and Marla, I'm very independent… it's in this safe environment, at Windsor Castle, where I have my awakening. We discover Scott and Marla's excitement to be magnetic. And, as we're surrounded by different individuals from all different walks of life – there is one common purpose, and objective; the Tree of Life… to shift consciousness. I realize the reason why I travel from Florida to London, is to participate in this Workshop and meet Scott and Marla, so I can have this awakening.

Richard:
We are all on different steps, and moments in the journey of life; within different stages; and yet, we still feel connected… as if we're on one big journey together. The phrase I emphasize prior to the retreat is "go big or go home." Following the retreat, the phrase changes to "be big and be home." This is a *mind-shift*.

Lisa:
I arrived at the realization that you're supposed to be wherever you are, and with the people you're with; and if something happens to get in your way, it's supposed to happen. If my team becomes anxious, I share with them that there is a solution to every problem; and we can figure it out. "So, let's not worry about making the solution perfect, let's focus on the solution; because, ultimately, it will work out."

Richard:
The Intention Stick helps you to focus on where you are in the present – and reassures "it's okay to be you." Life is not always a

competition, and not always a game. The Intention of *Be, Let It Be* in the Intention Stick helps produce a huge shift in the minds of people I speak with; and many stories, experiences, feelings, and emotions are all wrapped around the Tree of Life Intention Stick.

My son borrows my Intention Stick, and misplaces it. So, I order a new one. The day it arrives, I drive three hours to Jeremy's funeral: my college roommate who passed away from a brain tumor; we played football in high school, and grew up together. Before leaving for the funeral, I select a word for my Intention Stick which I feel that I need at this moment. I'm not sure why, but I'm immediately drawn to this particular word.

When I arrive, I find out the funeral is a 'celebration of life ceremony' for Jeremy's passing. In the middle of the ceremony, Jeremy's twin brother, Matt, looks directly at me and says, "Jeremy wants everyone to simply choose *joy*." On his deathbed, Jeremy is still courageously giving, and encouraging his family and friends around him with the Intention of *Joy*.

"Holy shift!" The intention I've chosen is *Happiness*. This is a real defining moment for me.

I realize that we have a choice: You can complain, you can argue, you can be unhappy; you can say, "Life's not fair – why me?" Or, you can simply choose the Intention of *Joy*, and be happy. What are the chances that Jeremy's ceremony, and celebration of life is based around the intention I chose prior to arriving?

It's easy to see how wearing the Intention Stick can affect people. It's a tool, and a reminder that you have a choice. And when you face a difficult decision, it allows you to choose the Intentions of *Happiness*, *Health*, *Be Let It Be*, or any intention which is important to you. And, for me, it's *Happiness*.

In my experience, the Intention Stick and being part of the Tree of Life Movement is giving yourself permission to take the next step in your journey without the feeling of guilt. This gives you the strength that you're not alone, and a significant reason to take a step forward with the peace of mind that everything will be okay.

OUR RETURN TO THE CASTLE (LEADING WITH HUMILITY)
– 11 –

Marla:

In November of 2019: Scott and I are invited as Leadership Fellows to Windsor Castle. The theme is "Leading With Humility," and there are sixteen inspirational leaders participating in this eventful gathering.

The first evening, we introduce ourselves (as a group) in St. George's Tea Room. A meeting follows in Vicars' Hall; where Pete Ashby, the program director, encourages each leadership fellow to share their own story of leading with humility. As Pete directs our attention to one another, this process of storytelling continues until each of us share …

Andrew, a high-tech CEO, acknowledges when his company has success, he likes to celebrate; and immediately, thereafter, he moves on – to the next project – to the next "mountain to climb."

At this moment, I feel inspired to share my thoughts about Andrew's story; "I believe it's important to take a breath; to check in with yourself, and be present."

"You have to celebrate and just keep going," Andrew says with conviction.

We seem to have opposing viewpoints for when to move forward, and how to approach the next project. Based on this conversation, Scott and I carefully consider how these next few days will unfold.

The following day, we separate into groups (of three people) in Vicars' Hall. Scott and I are in different groups, yet our experiences are quite similar. As Scott and I share our experiences with one another, it seems as if each person, in both of our groups, is interested to hear about the Tree of Life Movement and the Intention Stick; however, in Scott's group, they seem to convey a skeptical point of view...

Two fellows, Andrew and a math professor, who participate in Scott's group, both emphasize, (after Scott shares the significance of *trusting* the journey), this skeptical viewpoint.

"How you can live your entire life around trust is beyond us," they share.

Because of Andrew's, and the professor's point of view, they have reluctance to connecting with Scott's overall message to trust the journey. The Intention of *Trust* is the one intention which (even when we change our intentions) always remains, and always will remain present, Scott shares.

After our individual-group conversations, each fellow gathers together; where Pete encourages Scott and I to share our story of the Tree of Life Movement, and the Intention Stick. When the meeting concludes, for an intermission of sorts, with tea and crumpets... upon returning, Scott notices Andrew approaching him with a puzzled look.

"I have to share something with you," Andrew affirms; "this dropped into my email in-box, post our conversation this afternoon, and it got through our spam filter. Nothing gets through our spam filter. I have no idea about the text within the email, but the title is "Trust – the one thing that changes everything." Your chosen word, when talking with us about the Intention Stick, was *Trust*. And this has freaked me out a little. Let's talk more tonight."

Pete shares with the group, because Scott and I feel inspired to gift each participant an Intention Stick, that "Scott and Marla would like to share their story about the the Tree of Life Movement;" from which, (some time later this evening), we gift everyone an Intention Stick.

As we hold hands as a group, to say a group blessing for setting intentions with our Intention Sticks, the priest of St. George's Cathedral joins the room.

Scott:

"We would be honored to gift you an Intention Stick."

"I would be honored," the priest says.

The priest receives an Intention Stick, joins the group, holds hands, and says the blessing of intention. We ask everyone to choose three intentions; any three intentions they feel they need, or are inspired to select … in this present moment.

Following the group blessing, I notice Andrew is sitting by a window. He seems to be contemplating; so I walk over to Andrew. "Is everything okay?" I ask.

"Not really. I only see two words: *Trust* and *Courage*."

"I really feel that your third intention is: *Be, Let It Be*."

Andrew feels that the two intentions he selects are perfect, and places the remaining list of intentions (inside his Intention Stick box) in his pocket. Five minutes following this conversation, I sit back down, next to Andrew, and ask: "Is everything okay?"

"My pocket is on fire!" Andrew says; "… after placing the remaining (twenty) intentions in my pocket. And the two intentions I'm seeing are: *Health* and *Be, Let It Be*."

"Be open to the messages," I suggest; "because if we can't learn to forgive, and let our past go with love, then what we hold onto will turn into sickness and disease."

Andrew places the two Intentions of H*ealth* and *Be, Let It Be* inside his Intention Stick. Andrew shares that this feeling of fire in his pocket has gone away, and that he's inspired to go for a walk.

I return to the reception ... when Andrew arrives, he sits next to me: Andrew shares, while he was on his walk, that he called his wife, and explained to her how he chose his intentions; and is starting to see this as an awakening.

Marla:

The next morning, is the last day of the retreat; and, as an exercise, Pete lays out three mats on the floor. As you step on the first mat, you're encouraged to affirm your vision of where you perceive yourself in three months. As you step on the second mat, is where you'll be in one year. And, on the third mat, two years.

"Who would like to go first?" Pete asks.

Scott and I raise our hands, and join Pete on the mats; which is an incredibly emotional, and enlightening experience, to proclaim where you're going to be – and, by way of affirmation, declaring where you will be!

Following our experience with this exercise, Andrew steps on the first mat. Andrew cries: "Three months from now, I am retiring. I will give my resignation being CEO of my company." Andrew steps onto the second mat, and affirms: "A year from now, I will have my replacement." And lastly, as Andrew stands on the third mat: "In two years, I will be managing the Tree of Life movement."

All of us are in tears, and are crying from this exceptionally powerful, (heartfelt, and endearing) moment ...

As the Leading with Humility retreat concludes, we form a group to stay in communication with one another. Andrew establishes the name of our group as, "Team TOLIS" – because of an acronym I shared with him – Team Tree of Life Intention Stick.

Meaningful Experiences
– 12 –

Scott:

O ur connections with people, (who continue to help evolve and expand the Tree of Life Movement), are continuously being strengthened in meaningful ways. We are experiencing the miracle of divine timing, and how this is taking root and growing globally...

Marla and I are visiting Tel Aviv, Israel. It's the the Jewish Sabbath. I walk over to the beach, while Marla is at the hotel. In the middle of the intersection, I hear a car horn – so, I turn around... and (twenty feet away from me...) a taxi pulls up to the light.

The taxi driver rolls down his window... "are you from the United States?" he asks.

"Yes," I say.

The driver introduces himself as Artur.

"My brother Danny and sister-in-law, Julie, live in Scottsdale," Artur says.

Julie and Danny recently sent an Intention Stick to Artur in Israel.

Artur sees that I'm wearing an Intention Stick, and he feels an instant affinity – as this seems to be happening everywhere, all around the world; when people who are wearing an Intention Stick encounter each other.

This is truly a gift; and, as we're fond of saying … no coincidence here!

* * *

Marla:

While George is visiting Arizona – and, yes, there is no coincidence! – someone tells him about the Intention Stick; so he decides that he needs one. I ask George to share his story …

Years ago … George is a part of the Canadian Olympic team; and being a part of the team, requires George to undergo a psychological evaluation. It involves having to write thirty things on a piece of paper that makes George happy. So, George writes his list, and hands it to the psychologist. The psychologist reads the list, then returns it back to George.

"Now, narrow this down to three things," the Psychologist says.

George narrows his list of the things that make him happy to these three:

Someone to love.
Something important to do.
Something to look forward to.

The psychologist reads this list and hands it back to George. "Live your life by those three things."

Many years have passed since George had his evaluation … George is cleaning out his lake house, and finds this list, and reads it to himself …

"I forgot," George says, "I completely forgot about those three things.

"You remind me of the story of *The Little Prince*," I say to George; "because it's not getting older that's the problem, it's forgetting."

George wants an Intention Stick for this purpose; "to remember those things I need in my life," George emphasizes.

THE HEARTBEAT WITHIN
– 13 –

Tom and Tracey Martin

*Tom: I have served in the field of construction
and building most of my life. My true focus is
building a strong foundation within myself
so I may be the rock for my family. To be the
example of the type of men, I want
in my daughters' future.*

*Tracey: As an Immersive Transformational
Coach, my heart is for the world. To be in service
to families and Generation Z. I believe being in
service to another person's growth in one of the
most rewarding and humble acts we can do.*

*A family rooted in foundational faith
will leave a lasting impact.*

Marla:

There's a common feeling within each person who wears an Intention Stick; as if it has its own heartbeat. This is to say, the Intention Stick becomes a part of you. "When wearing it over your heart and holding hands with a group of people, all of whom are standing in a circle, it feels as if there's one heartbeat," as Tom and Tracey are inspired to share.

Tracey:
The Intention Stick that I wear over my heart, never leaves me. So many times, I've been asked, "What is that? It caught my eye…"

"I'm so glad you asked," I say; because now I can share the meaning and story with them.

Sometimes people don't seem ready to hear the message until they are open enough to receive, and hear the underlying purpose. I've gifted so many, and I always keep at least one or two Intention Sticks with me, just in case…

When someone asks about the Intention Stick I'm wearing, it's an opportunity. So, I sit down with them, and say, "since you've noticed mine, I'd like to gift this to you. And I explain that; that the Intention Stick is my grounding tool. It's my compass."

Tom:
When the intentions are inside, it's almost as if you're putting on armor.

… It's your personal armor.

And, right now, with what's going on in the world, whichever intention you select – or whichever intentions you wear – there is a positivity and an energy that comes from it, which you can actually feel.

A Guiding Hand
(For You and Me)
– 14 –

Marla:

It's November of 2017, Jaden, our youngest daughter, is studying (classical) piano with Larry Clapp; an exceptionally talented pianist who studied classical piano at the Juilliard School, performed with the Tucson, Mesa, and Phoenix Symphonies, and, in 2002, performed at Carnegie Hall.

We develop a strong connection with Larry, (through the years our children have been practicing piano with him). In addition, because of our meaningful conversations, Larry shares with me some personal insights; one of which, is that he has diabetes.

I recognize Larry is having a difficult time (more than usual) sitting and standing from his chair. At this time, Larry also shares with Jaden and I that his son has been getting himself into questionable situations. He's very concerned about his son ... and this seems to be weighing on Larry; spiritually, emotionally, and physically.

So, I share with Jaden, "I think it's time we gift Larry an Intention Stick."

Larry is a passionate and heartfelt individual, a spiritual and endearing man, and is immensely compassionate for everyone around him. And his devotion to his family, friends, and students is implicit.

"Jaden and I have a gift for you. And there's a story with the gift that we would like to share, if you can please leave us with some extra time next week during Jaden's lesson."

When we return the following week for Jaden's piano lesson, I share the story of the Intention Stick with Larry, the symbolic meaning of the Tree of Life, and the intention of selecting positive intentions.

Larry is such a loving father, and he cares so much about his son. "Your son is on his journey," I share, "and because it's his journey, he will figure it out – just like you and I have … if you let him make his own choices, he will learn from them."

The consequences of our choices and actions (whether negative or positive) are, ultimately, great lessons. Larry seems to be processing what I'm sharing; "it's okay to love yourself."

"Can you please help me choose my words for the Intention Stick?" Larry asks. So, Jaden and I help Larry select his intentions: *Health, Love,* and *Be, Let It Be* and place them inside his Intention Stick. As we attempt to clasp the chain around Larry's neck, we notice that it's too short.

"I'm so sorry. Please hold on to your Intention Stick, and place it in your pocket," I say. "When we come back this week for Jaden's lesson, I will bring you the appropriate chain." This is on Sunday, November 12, 2017.

Jaden and I drive back on Tuesday with a brand-new chain, and I'm feeling exceptionally enthusiastic. This time, when I try to clasp Larry's Intention Stick around his neck, for some reason, the clasp will not work. I'm embarrassed; "I'm so sorry, I don't know what's going on?"

After I walk to my car to see if I can fix the chain, I walk back inside Larry's house … "I promise" to Larry that "when I come back next week, the chain will clasp. Please keep the

Intention Stick with you, nearby; the blessings of Intention will be there to guide you."

November 15, 2017, Larry sends the following text message: "wanted to thank you so, so very much for the beautiful gift!….It means a great deal to me and I will cherish it with all my heart….I think I will wait for you to find a proper chain….I would really like for you to put it on me, rather than put it on myself….it would be very meaningful to me….I send my love to all of you."

Now, I'm on a mission; the next chain is going to work; the next chain will, in fact, work. Jaden and I are on our way to Larry's house for Jaden's weekly piano lesson; and, as soon as we arrive at the front door, we see a note attached: "There's been a family emergency, please call this number." So, I call the number and Larry's ex-wife answers the phone. She says that "Larry passed away."

Larry transitioned November 16, 2017, early in the morning, following the day, and night after Larry sent me the message. For a few days thereafter, I am really distraught. I'm thinking to myself: "If only I got there sooner…if only I got the Intention Stick on him…maybe this would have helped Larry."

As I am processing all of this information, our four children emphasize the same message to me, which is: "The Intention Stick was never meant to go around Larry's neck – it happened exactly the way it was meant to be." I finally connected with this message; that Jaden and I were there to help Larry transition with some peace, love, and compassion for himself, and for his son.

Our Rabbi, who is a very spiritual man, invites Jaden and I to his home, so I can share this story and message about Larry.

"This is one of God's winks; this is a profound message for you," the Rabbi endearingly says.

I miss Larry for many reasons; and one of them is because of the strong connection he shared with both my family and I. We constantly have conversations about Larry. And I would like to believe that Jaden and I were able to encourage and help Larry in some way or another; by being there with him, when he needed a guiding hand.

(In Loving Memory of Larry Clapp)

THE GIFT OF INTENTION
– 15 –

Scott:

Our dear friend Mark (physically and spiritually) invests in 100 Intention Sticks, so he can gift them when he's inspired. "I don't know who they are for ... " Mark says, "but I know when they come into my life, it will be for this reason." Only a few days later, he sends this message to Marla and I, via text, December 19, 2017:

> "Scott and Marla, I am just walking out of the mental ward at Banner Hospital, visiting a friend's fifteen-year-old daughter, who has been struggling with issues that popped up out of nowhere this year. She is such an amazing kid and this hit everyone as a huge surprise when she broke down. I was quietly asking her what a fifteen-year-old would think of an Intention Stick. She is not very easy to talk to, and very rarely opens up. But she explained to me why she needed inspiration and trust right now.
>
> As I was leaving the room her Mom came up to me crying, asking how I got her to open up. The daughter had been speaking and trusting me in a way she never would have without such a strong tool. Each time I

have given an Intention Stick, the gift has gone to me, knowing I just passed along a miracle. I told the girl the only thing I ask for in return is that she shares her story when she sees it working. Nobody gets one for free. Real magic!"

* * *

What if one day you were stripped of everything. Your home, your clothes, everything. What's left? It's just people ... – at the end of the day, when our time comes, everybody's going to be the same. It doesn't matter what color you are, or the diseases you've had, everybody will be the same. Even if we affect just one extra life, it means the world. Just one extra life, and it could save a life.

Scott:

This is Pete and Richelle Nassos's philosophy about being of service to others. Like so many beautiful souls within our ever-growing Tree of Life Movement family, Richelle and Pete wear their Intention Sticks as they pursue their dedication to help other people in need. They manufacture, and distribute first aid and health products around the world; and, for nearly two decades, they have been employing 300 disabled persons in the U.S. – rather than being outside of the U.S. Because, doing so makes a difference in so many people's lives.

Following our conversation with Pete and Richelle, after they each receive their Intention Sticks, they send Marla and I this beautiful, heartfelt message:

As I'm sure you'll agree, we could have talked through-out the night. Quite frankly, we are still digesting and discussing what had taken place. A purpose. A purpose of who we are, why we are here and what God expects from us as we are HIS tools to emulate him. Just this morning while in our bible study, we were just discussing the heart and how our actions and words that come from our lips define who we are and how we treat others and our true INTENTIONS. Then we meet with the 2 of you? REALLY? OH HOW HE WORKS, if we would just listen.

25 years I have known you and have known you to always be the person you are today. Maybe this has been your calling, your calling to teach others about a force we all have but yet not know how to use and use properly. This is a movement and one that will erupt into something larger than life. I'm sure you're seeing this, it's that we're seeing it too. Maybe God is calling you to be a modern day Moses and Zipporah? God calls all of us, you just listened.

You stated Marla's words when you gave her the first tree, stating that she was done. You had everything. Richelle and I discussed this as well when we left. We have our 3 boys, we are all healthy, have a roof over our heads, cars, our own business, we make a difference in the lives of the disabled and our marriage was meant to be. We are blessed. Our thoughts moving forward are to tell others as you have told us.

We'll be in touch soon enough and in the meantime if you need any advice as to scaling up (because you'll need it) we're always here for you.

God bless the both you, your children, your staff and all who surround you.

With love,
Pete & Richelle

"Life is a journey, it's about the people you meet and lives you touch along the way." You are doing just that.

* * *

Scott:

A philosophy which Marla and I truly resonate with, is one that Josh, a dear friend of ours, opens our eyes to…

Josh is the head of a global company; and one of the projects, and services to the world he attends to, is he helps build wells in Third World countries.

When we share the story of the Intention Stick with Josh, he's truly inspired… following our conversation, Josh calls Marla and I, and shares an incredibly heartfelt voice message:

"Can you please overnight another Intention Stick for my dear friend in New York? She's going through a wrenching breakup; her ex-husband physically abused her in horrific ways," Josh shares; and continues, "If we think about it, everyone in the world right now is walking wounded. Everyone is going through something. Everyone needs, and can use an Intention Stick. This is our opportunity to help as many people as possible."

* * *

Scott:

It's December 2018, and 'being guided' is the theme of our first conversation with Jennifer Solomon. Jennifer is a philanthropist and community volunteer, who visits our gallery, with a ring she's inspired to redesign.

Jennifer notices that I wear a Tree of Life bracelet, and shares with me how much she loves everything about the Tree of Life symbol. At this moment, it seems to me that Jennifer is being guided to our jewelry gallery so she can receive an Intention

Stick… Jennifer chooses the following intentions to place in her Intention Stick: *Knowledge, Trust* and *Peace*.

Jennifer and her husband Steven have two daughters. She explains to Marla and I about her long standing desire to have another child; and to gift her husband with a son so they can carry on his name and legacy… having a son as their third child, is in Jennifer's mind and thoughts.

Jennifer receives miraculous news. Within a matter of weeks following our conversation with Jennifer, she shares with Marla and I that wearing the Intention Stick has helped her to open up, and let go of energy which seems to have been blocking them from conceiving another child. Marla and I are truly grateful.

When Steven and Jennifer's third child is born, they ask Marla and I to bless their son, spiritually, with an intention ceremony. Their extended family joined this beautiful ceremony, and they gifted each of them with an Intention Stick. This incredible moment with their family, and their newborn son, is, in our eyes, an exceptionally memorable and meaningful experience.

TIKKUN OLAM
– 16 –

A dynamic shift of consciousness from lower to higher, (from negative to positive), strengthens our state of awareness with a positive point of view; which is to say, shifting consciousness from a lower point of view which is negative, to a higher point of view which is positive, (from negative to positive), thus strengthens our state of awareness.

Strengthening our state of awareness, is as intentional as letting go of a painful memory and experience (from childhood or any period of time which creates negative thoughts and emotions); as to forgive, surrender to, and let go of our negative thoughts and emotions; in a positive way.

The guiding aspect to forgive, surrender, and let go is the *approach-perspective-outcome* of our past, present, and future points of view. We forgive our past as our approach. We surrender to our present as our perspective. And, we let go, so we can attend to the outcome of our future.

If we don't learn how to forgive, surrender to, and let go of our painful memories and experiences with the Intentions of *Love, Health, Courage*, (or any positive intention which resonates with us in the present moment), then our negative thoughts will continue to cause and, thus, create negative emotions within us ...

Because our emotions are based on our thoughts, our positive thoughts create positive emotions, and negative thoughts create negative emotions: all of which lead to their corresponding effect, either negative or positive. So, based on our thoughts and emotions, they act and play an important role in both positive and negative aspects. This is to say, moments based on a positive approach, positive thoughts and feelings, (thinking about happy and joyful occasions, memories and experiences), bring about a positive perspective; thus, lead to a positive outcome. And, this is to say, moments based on a negative approach, negative thoughts and feelings, (thinking about sad and painful occasions, memories and experiences), bring about a negative perspective; thus, lead to a negative outcome.

Over many years, Marla and I have spent time connecting, speaking, and working with various medical doctors, physicians, and healers around the world. Upon which it has been consistently shared with us that by surgically removing a disease, i.e. cancer, or treating it with chemotherapy, radiation, or both, can (or, in some cases, will) result in the cancer reemerging with a far more serious intensity, and vengeance; based on unresolved emotions – i.e. emotional ties to either one or multiple painful memories and experiences.

Because negative thoughts and emotions do not serve us for the better, allowing ourselves to be open and present with self and others helps create this positive shift of consciousness. From which we experience the presence and state of awareness we are inspired by and aspire to experience.

Positive intention is a way to shift into a more present, more meaningful state of awareness; for healthier, and stronger connections and experiences. This unifying aspect that positive intention instills within us, is the ability to bring ourselves into the present moment with enthusiasm – with a positive, heartfelt, and endearing point of view.

As we learn how to let go of our painful thoughts and emotions, the act of forgiving, surrendering, and letting go will help us create our positive thoughts and emotions. As we move away from our negative thoughts and emotions, this will help us heal; as we move upward, onward, and forward, toward positive thoughts and emotions.

* * *

Scott:

When I receive messages about someone, I feel inspired (and guided); to connect with them... the thought of Tony comes to mind in my morning meditation; so, in this moment, I call Tony.

I ask Tony to meet me at my office. And, when Tony arrives, I share with him a few of the stories Marla and I have been experiencing with the Tree of Life Movement – the miracles people have been experiencing, as they wear their Intention Stick.

Tony, who appears to be, in almost every sense, well built, strong, and resilient, begins to cry.

"I didn't mean to make you cry," I say.

"No, you don't understand; the words you're speaking are verbatim from the book of Kabbalah."

I've never opened the book of Kabbalah; because in Judaism, unless you become an Orthodox Rabbi, and study for forty years, it's not the case that you should open or study the book of Kabbalah.

Tony lives in L.A., and studies at the Kabbalah center. He is a very mathematical, logical, and scientific individual. Tony is not a religious person; although, he's truly a spiritual person.

After holding Tony's Intention Stick, saying the intentional blessing, and asking for blessings of health, Tony opens up his Intention Stick, chooses his intentions, and seals them inside. Now, I place the Intention Stick around his neck...

Tony immediately starts crying.

I see all of the color flow back into Tony's face.

"It just left – it's gone!"

"What's gone? What just left?" I emphasize.

"All of the pain in my body just left," Tony exclaims.

Tony starts moving his arms around – to show me how he can move his arms, freely, with ease, and without discomfort.

Tony explains:

"Scott, you don't understand, I couldn't even get out of bed this morning, because I was in so much pain. I don't even like to take an ibuprofen for my pain, but something was telling me I must come in to see you."

Tony continues; "because of the words I chose, with a pure heart, coming from pure love, and pure intention, and the fact that you gave this to me as a gift, expecting nothing in return, this healed me. And I say that as the biggest skeptic in the world. Originally, I was resistant to come in and meet with you; because I thought you were trying to sell me something. I've been dealing with the pain of Lyme Disease for many years ... "

And now, I'm crying, because I'm witnessing a miracle in front of my eyes.

I sit down to compose myself.

After Tony leaves, I'm still trying to process what happened. So, I call Marla. "I don't think I understand what's going on," I say; "I just witnessed this miracle."

Marla and I call our "rockstar" Rabbi. He is someone you generally do not envision as an Orthodox Rabbi; the typical painted picture is a Rabbi with a substantial beard, who's wearing a black hat. Our Rabbi is from Cape Town, South Africa, plays rugby, becomes an MMA fighter, competes and completes an Ironman (triathlon), and is a brilliant mind within the IT world and tech industry. Hence, rockstar Rabbi.

Marla and I share with him Tony's story, and all of the miraculous stories that we have witnessed up to this point. Now he starts to cry; this is one thing you don't want to do … which is make a Priest or Rabbi cry. "Rabbi, we didn't mean to make you cry," I say.

"Scott and Marla, the words you're speaking and sharing with me are verbatim from the book of the Talmud."

The book of the Talmud is the older righteous Rabbis debating the Old Testament in the Torah, which I've never opened to study – because it's written in Hebrew.

The Rabbi proceeds to tell us that the message Marla and I received with the Tree of Life Intention Stick is well over 3,000 years old, from Holy Scripture.

"This is what you've tapped into;" as he explains to us how today, in this world, "there are two doors: a door of good and a door of evil."

"We all have the ability to open either one, and walk through. What you've been given has opened a third smaller door that is more powerful than good and evil combined. Not only will it heal the soul of the world. It will heal everyone within it. … This is Tikkun Olam," the Rabbi says.

* * *

We believe that we must continue to love ourselves with true unconditional love, so we can help heal each other and the world; and, therefore, so we can love our brothers and sisters as we love ourselves.

HO'OPONOPONO
PRACTICE OF RECONCILIATION
AND FORGIVENESS MEDITATION
– 17 –

Marty Haberer

*Marty is the President & CEO of the
Jewish Federation of Greater Phoenix. He is a
husband, a father, a son, a brother and an Uncle.
His goal in life is to be remembered as a mensch.*

I'm constantly feeling the positive energy of the Intention Stick; and whether I'm bringing this energy to myself, or others, I believe the Intention Stick is quite remarkable.

An Intention Stick reminds me of the same elements of what a mezuzah has when it's placed on a door. Every time I see one on a doorpost, I always kiss the mezuzah; because, for me, the act of kissing the mezuzah is a reminder that there is something bigger than me controlling everything. It's about being grateful and acknowledging that power. So, for me, carrying an Intention Stick is literally like carrying a doorpost on your heart all the time.

When you summon your inner strength to intention, it's about *focus*. Scott and Marla, in many ways, changed my life when they introduced me to this wonderful Talisman they created, which I wear over my heart; and then these incredible things, and experiences start happening. There are a number of interesting experiences which continue to happen to me; as I focus my energies, not just on the intentions I need, but, in addition, on the intentions I want for others.

One of these stories, and experiences is … I'm having a couple of exceptionally stressful days at work while I'm trying to fill a position; so, I select the word, *Success*. As I walk out to the front of my office, I overhear someone in the reception area. They're talking about how they want to relocate to Scottsdale and are looking for a position; exactly the one I need to fill … and, sure enough, this individual is now General Director.

Another story which guides me to the Intention of *Blessed*, occurs because a donor has written a substantial check which doesn't clear, and this places us in a financial bind. I'm having a very challenging day; so, I select the intention, *Blessed*, and leave my office. When I come back, the phone rings … it's the donor. The donor apologizes for this misunderstanding and offers to immediately send over the donation.

My experience with this nasty case of sciatica, leads me to the Intention of *Health*. I'm limping around my home with back pain and can hardly move. I'm looking for my intentions, so I can change my words in my Intention Stick. I find the intentions, and place the Intention of *Health* in there, and immediately feel better.

I share this story, and the pain I've been dealing with Marla and Scott. And Marla expresses to me that I ought to be telling myself more often that "I love myself." Scott also shares with me about the Ho'oponopono practice of reconciliation and forgiveness meditation; and to *focus* on certain key intentions in combination with the will to heal myself. Now, two and a half months later, I am 95 percent cured of this nasty sciatica I've been feeling.

It becomes clear to me: If you really don't like yourself, or love yourself, then how can you expect other people to like, or love you? It's not just about loving other people; it's also about loving yourself. I can say that 'I'm a great guy;' yet, if I don't really believe this, then who else should believe it? Or, why else should someone believe it? It must start with me believing this – first! – and not in a prideful way; but in an objective manner.

One of the gifts of this pandemic, is that it forced us inside, and not just inside our homes; but in a sense, learning that it's okay to be inside with ourselves. We've had an opportunity to recalibrate a lot of things, and therefore learn to know ourselves better; which has helped us change a lot of our old habits.

I believe the power of the Intention Stick works, as we bring the power of positive intention into our lives. It's very important to *focus* on the fact that this is not just for us individually; but, also, to mirror it out into the collective.

NOTE TO READER
FROM SCOTT AND MARLA

* * *

Marla:

A t the time, when Scott and I see Marty, prior to him feeling "95 percent cured," I ask Marty: "Why do you think you are only 85 percent better? What are you holding onto?" After Marty processes this, this reminds Marty of an adverse experience, when he was in college:

While Marty is in college, his car is constantly getting broken into. Eventually, Marty finds his car with both a broken window and a stolen radio. Insurance sends Marty a check for $3,500, and it only costs him $1,500 for the repairs and new radio. He tells the person who repaired his car to keep the whole check, that is, the entirety of it.

When Marty shares this story with Scott and I about his experience in college, and about his experience with back pain from sciatica, I share with Marty that, because he is constantly giving of himself to others in such a meaningful and caring way, where, and when, he attends to others more than he attends to himself (most times); that he is *The Giving Tree*.

Scott:

The Hawaiian *Ho'oponopono* practice of reconciliation and forgiveness meditation is an intentional meditative practice to affirm forgiveness in order to bring yourself into a more loving environment, mental state of awareness for inner *peace* and *healing*, and thus *loving* self.

As this practice suggests: to continue this reconciliation and forgiveness meditative journey of your inner fears, anxieties, and stresses; to not turn around, go back, and look at the past; to *be, let it be,* and thus continue, onward, upward, and forward, as you move toward a more loving, inner self. This is a personal, four-step self-exploration, which affirms:

> *I'm sorry.*
> *Please forgive me.*
> *Thank you.*
> *I love you.*

I'M HEALED!

– 18 –

Mark and Isabel Candelaria

Mark is Founding Partner of Candelaria Design,
a chef, blogger, podcast host and traveler. Isabel
is Senior Interior Designer of Earth and Images, a
spiritual teacher and traveler. They
have three daughters.

Isabel:

When I was introduced to Scott and Marla and the Intention Stick, I had been diagnosed with two different types of cancer:

At this time, I'm having profound, spiritual experiences. I feel divinely guided to come to their office. And I do believe the Intention Stick is like the symbol, or the catalyst that infiltrates everything that I'm experiencing.

Mark:

For me, I was going through so much uncertainty:

We don't know what's around the corner, and we have plenty of next-corners thrown at us during this period. I'm looking for every opportunity to gather positive, healing energy; and, wherever I can gather and find it to support Isabel, I'm going for it.

It's just a great experience to be with Scott and Marla, and feel their energy. We select our words, Health, *Faith*, and *Courage*, for our Intention Sticks; and, several times, we get chills from feeling their energy. Isabel and I both walk out of this meeting, feeling very relieved and peaceful, saying to ourselves: "We've received some more positive energy. Let's just keep going."

And this keeps us moving in the right direction.

Isabel:

When I see Scott and Marla, I'm in a state of complete surrender about everything, and the right experiences are coming to me. The Intention Stick is a symbol of God's plan for my life.

As Scott and Marla like to share:
What makes God laugh?
It's telling God your plans.
Because we're always being guided.

The Intention Stick is a symbol of being mindful about where you choose to place your focus: on *health*, on wellness, on prosperity, or *peace*. It's a symbol you can physically handle – a reminder you feel as you wear it over your heart. This is a symbol of the intention your mind is focused on, so you can stay present with yourself.

Mark:

Surrender is true for me too. We've come to a point when we both acknowledge this is in God's hands. Whatever is meant to be is meant to happen. And we're going to do everything on our side, so we can fulfill God's destiny. Receiving the Intention Stick, and meeting Scott and Marla is part of this experience.

And, since then, I think we've really tried to maintain this philosophy; nothing is certain. It's up to God what happens; yet we can do our part to make certain it's toward light, and not toward darkness.

Isabel has been diagnosed with cancer. Now we have a choice: We can either surrender and let cancer consume us, and that's the end of it; or we can fight, and we can pray, and do things that are positive for all of humanity to make it a better world. And then, we can be healed. This is to say, we can be healed if we choose to be healed.

Everyone is going through something. I don't care if you're rich, poor, or polka-dotted, it doesn't matter. We all have to be a lot more compassionate, and listen to the shoes others walk in. We've all lost track of the importance of this. Everything we're trying to do is not that difficult, we're just overcomplicating it. What's next, is still in our control – if we let God's energy infuse our decision-making, there's going to be a much better outcome than what we've been seeing.

I call this the ripple effect; because you drop a little pebble in a pond, and it can grow – it just takes off. It's just endless energy, if you let it go in that direction; the reverse is also true. It's the little acts of kindness along the way, each day, that make a huge difference when it's all added up. Each individual needs to take the initiative to say: "Today I'm going to focus on love and compassion. I'm not going to let any evil and negativity come into my heart."

Isabel:

I learned that sometimes, previously, before going through cancer, I was a little sloppy with my words and affirmations, compared to when I was going through cancer. When I was going through cancer, I would literally say, every morning: "This may be the last thing I'm going to do, I better do it the best I can."

During that time, I think there were only three days when I didn't take a shower and get ready for the day. Although I might not feel like doing anything, I would still be ready. In the afternoon, if I had one or two hours of energy, I would accomplish something. And, I would be ready when Mark got home from work. I had my best saved for him, too.

My philosophy is simple. Do your life well. And, if you're overextended, pull back, and really focus on what you're doing; and thus, do it really well – with the right intention. This philosophy has been a gift that I've received from my experience. I'm so much happier living my life this way.

NOTE TO READER FROM SCOTT AND MARLA

* * *

Scott:

We're compelled to share the backstory of how we meet Mark and Isabel.

November 2017, on a Friday afternoon, our office doorbell rings. A couple arrives unexpectedly; and would like an insurance replacement for their jewelry.

Nancy notices the bracelet on my wrist, and asks, "is that the symbol of the Tree of Life?"

"Yes!" I exclaim.

"Ever since childhood, I've been infatuated with the Tree of Life," Nancy emphasizes.

We have a deep conversation with them; and, being a meeting which should've lasted only thirty minutes, because they arrive in search of an insurance replacement, Tom and Nancy stay in our office, in conversation with us, for nearly two hours…

This insightful conversation leads to many different avenues and topics; yet maintaining a common thread about life, positive intention; and, in relation to what becomes a substantial part of this conversation, how each part of the body has a philosophical (metaphysical) meaning. This is to say, when pain or illness arises in certain parts of the body, a philosophical (metaphysical) message underlies the pain or illness.

At first, Tom is averse to our conversation; and to philosophical messages, which underly pain or illness in the body; and emphasizes in a playfully sarcastic way; "woo-woo! I'm going to win the lotto."

Nancy, on the other hand, is the complete opposite. She is perfectly open-minded, optimistic, and views life with a point of view that stems from the Tree of Life.

Marla and I share that these experiences of pain and these experiences of illness both arise in the body in a spiritual and philosophical way; and thus, show up for a reason. This pain or illness is there to guide us, and to share that there is an underlying aspect deeply rooted within us; which we may be ignoring, dismissing, or avoiding.

Based on this conversation, why we receive messages, and why we receive messages in relation to different aspects of our body (in view of present experiences, and memories of our past), Tom becomes more open to this conversation, and begins to share some personal insights with Marla and I…

Tom shares that he's been feeling pain in three distinct parts of his body: his knee, his shoulder, and his back… this is when Tom starts to view things (the pain he's experiencing) in a different way, from a different lens; and he becomes interested to find deeper meaning within the pain he's experiencing, and feeling… to discern whether self-reflection will help him connect with something he's potentially ignoring, dismissing, or avoiding.

We share the point of view that looking within, (to find deeper meaning), is to contemplate that everything in life (our experiences, connections, and ultimately our journey) has an underlying reason; from which everything works out accordingly, i.e. the way it's supposed to.

Near the end of our conversation is when we gift Tom and Nancy with Intention Sticks ... the next day, Marla and I receive an email; not from Nancy, but from Tom. Whereupon Tom shares with us, in this email and follow up phone call, that as they leave our office, from the elevator to the first floor, they encounter their dear friend, Mark Candelaria – who is pleasantly surprised, and asks Tom and Nancy why they're here!

"We've been upstairs meeting with Scott and Marla about an insurance replacement for our jewelry ... " Tom and Nancy share; which they proceed to ask ... "how's Isabel doing?"

"Isabel is finishing her second to last round of chemo," Mark says.

Tom and Nancy hold their Intention Sticks up to encourage Mark and Isabel to schedule an appointment with us ...

On Sunday, Mark and Isabel join us at our office and we gift them Intention Sticks. From which we share with Mark and Isabel the journey we've been on; how everything in life is a gift; and, yes, some of these gifts are difficult to receive ... because these gifts also arrive in the form of pain, tragedy, or sickness. Yet, all of these gifts, in any form, painful or not, ultimately lead us to the next step, and to the next destination in our life; yet, it's not about the destination ... it's about the journey.

We hold hands, to do an intention blessing ceremony, and both Mark and Isabel select their intentions. Scott places Isabel's Intention Stick around her neck, and Marla places Mark's Intention Stick around his; from which ...

Isabel affirms, "I'm healed!"

THE UNIVERSE MIRRORS
YOUR INTENTIONS
– 19 –

Dr. Beth Dupree

*Beth is a breast cancer surgeon, focused on
patient's healing journeys, and Vice President
of Surgical Services at Holy Redeemer Health
System. Medical Director of Oncology Services,
Founder of The Healing Consciousness Foundation,
and author of The Healing Consciousness.*

The phone call I receive from my best friend's mother is to inform me that my best friend is in the ICU. She is being read her last rites by a priest. And the mother asks; if I would like to say goodbye to her.

I bring an Intention Stick with me to the hospital; and the four words I select, and place inside the Intention Stick are *Love*, *Health*, *Oneness*, and *Believe*. After placing the Intention Stick around her neck, miraculously, the vital signs immediately improve, and she starts coming back to life. She has become stronger, and stronger. And, today, thankfully, she is healthy.

You can't make these amazing stories up... I'm always inspired to have eleven Intention Sticks with me, so I can gift them to my friends, co-workers, and patients.

One of my patients in Pennsylvania, is a nurse with breast cancer. Her limbs were amputated, because of a horrible infection. So, I placed the words *Health, Believe*, and *Oneness* into an Intention Stick and sent it to her. After her sisters put it on her, miraculously, she survived. When these miracles happen, you're looking around for Rod Serling, or someone, because you think you're in a *Twilight Zone* episode.

As a physician, surgeon, and scientist, I know a lot of people think this is woo-woo stuff. But, what I would suggest is: your thought forms, and beliefs guide your life. I always tell my patients: You either have fear or love, and it's a choice. The opposite of love is fear; and when you're in fear, you're bringing everything down to a place where it's kind of random and haphazard. When you raise your vibration into love, set an A+ intention to be an optimist, and you're seeing positive things and outcomes in your life, you're manifesting them; and bringing them back into your life, as the universe mirrors your intentions.

I've always tried to live my life with intention; because when you do, you're exactly in the moment, not looking in the rearview mirror, bemoaning what happened yesterday; and not so focused on something in the future that you can't yet touch. You're actually, physically, present in the moment.

When I decided to move from Pennsylvania to Sedona, Arizona, I set the intention to build a breast cancer center. I set a three-to-five-year timeline for the move, and everything fell into place. I set the intention that my purpose is to move to Sedona, cure cancer, and help people find healing. And, now, we are creating the Sedona Integrated Health Center.

This is the difference between either living your life with passion, purpose, and intention; or living your life as though it's nothing more than a random series of events.

Live with intention – and the best way to start is to create the opportunity. Sometimes I have five words in my Intention Stick, because I'm going to a meeting and these are the intentions I need to have; and I need to be able to have this process of setting the intention. This is what the Intention Stick does. It makes you become more intentional about how you live. This is a beautiful vessel, and the Tree of Life is about planting the seeds of your intention into everything that you do, and thus into your path forward in life.

NOTE TO READER
FROM SCOTT AND MARLA

* * *

Scott:

January 1st, 2018, Marla, our daughter Jaden, and I are in Sedona, and we want to gift an Intention Stick to our dear friend Lisa Dahl – at one of her beautiful restaurants, "Mariposa." We meet Lisa on Sunday for lunch. When we arrive at her restaurant, we find out Lisa's running an hour behind schedule, and we should begin lunch without her.

We share our journey of the Tree of Life Movement and the Intention Stick with Lisa when she arrives. The four of us hold hands, and do blessings. Lisa chooses her intentions, and begins to cry after she puts on her Intention Stick.

"You need to meet my dear friend, Dr. Beth Dupree. She is a very spiritual person, and I would like to connect you," Lisa offers. Mere seconds passing us by, and Dr. Beth Dupree walks up to our table. We find ourselves laughing at the beautiful connection that comes from Lisa manifesting this intention.

Lisa suggests that Dr. Dupree hear the story of the Tree of Life Movement and receive an Intention Stick. We share an intention blessing ceremony with Dr. Dupree, and gift her an Intention Stick. Dr. Dupree shares; she's just finished writing and editing her new book, and would love to gift each of us a copy of "The Healing Consciousness". Our miraculous story with Dr. Dupree continues to get better, and better, each and every day.

The way in which Dr. Dupree winds up at Mariposa ...

Originally, Dr. Dupree went to Pisa Lisa (which is one of Lisa Dahl's restaurants) for gelato, dulce de leche, however, it's unavailable.

So, Pisa Lisa sends Dr. Dupree to Mariposa; for dulce de leche ...
The timing is serendipitous!

STEPPING INTO YOUR FUTURE
– 20 –

Tiffany Corrina Cramer

Tiffany is a loving, caring, quick-witted funny,
smart, universal intelligent,
compassionate Hummingbird Warrior.

My first interaction with Scott and Marla is at their office, and my intention is to have Scott design me an engagement ring. I look down at Scott's bracelet and see an image of the Tree of Life. I've been infatuated with the Tree of Life since I was a little girl. Scott and Marla look at each other, smile, and say, "You're not just here for a ring design ... "

Scott and Marla share their story of the Intention Stick, the message behind it, and the twenty-two intentions. My eyes fill with tears. "This is why I'm here. Because my family and I need this right now."

My brother just passed away, a month ago, from a drug overdose. I also lost my Dad, from a heroin addiction. He once shared with me: "Tiffany, I will never love you more than I love heroin." I never went down that path. My brother did – because he desperately wanted our father's love.

You can say, I come from a family of lost souls. There was no sense of grounding when I was growing up: we moved nine times in one year. And, as an adult, I've jumped from one job to another; because I was looking for something, there was a void, and I didn't know what it was. I didn't realize this until recently, after I injured my hips. And since then, I've had both of my hips repaired.

Marla shares with me that the spiritual meaning of the hip is about moving forward in life. The hips are about stepping into your future. All of the trauma I've been carrying has been in my hips; especially because there was a lot of abuse in my childhood. There was a grandfather who did some things to me for seven years.

I usually keep the Intentions of *Health*, *Peace*, and *Courage* in my Intention Stick; because these are the intentions I need, when I feel really lost.

Three weeks from the day I received my Intention Stick, I called Scott:

"I need another Intention Stick for a dear friend, whose son, Brad, is in a coma. He has been in the hospital, in a coma, for three months, and has been experiencing heart problems." Scott confers with Marla, and she recommends that my friend places the words *Health*, *Love*, *Laugh*, and *Joy* into the Intention Stick. She suggests *Laugh* and *Joy* – because he has heart problems, and needs these intentions in his life.

Scott explains to me, when the father places the Intention Stick containing those words around his son's neck, he will also receive all of the blessings and intentions from the collective: from the tens of thousands of people already wearing them around the world. That evening, my friend places the Intention Stick around his son's neck. The next morning, Brad awakens from his three-month coma!

As if this isn't miraculous enough, it's not the end of this remarkable story. Not long after, Scott is watching a live video on Facebook of someone he knows: in this video, Kim is having a conversation with a young man who's in a wheelchair, appears to have Cerebral Palsy (CP); because of the way he gestures, and speaks seems consistent with the general symptoms. Scott says that he can feel the love and energy from this video. So, he calls Kim and asks her about the beautiful soul with CP.

"No, he doesn't have Cerebral Palsy," Kim clarifies; "he has been in a coma for several months."

Scott realizes that Kim is talking about Brad, who I gifted an Intention Stick to, through his father, and wakes up from being in a coma. Scott shares with me that Kim encourages him to share this story with Brad and his father. So, when Scott and Marla spend time with Brad and his father at their home, they share the story, and hold hands to do a blessing for Brad's continued *health*. I ask for signs left and right, and this is certainly one of them. There seems to be no coincidences with signs; Marla's birthday is also the same day as my mother's.

For all the lost souls out there: You know when you're a lost soul, when you don't feel grounded, and don't feel anything. Yet, just because you've had a bad childhood, or have lived in the hood – and I've lived in a lot of hoods – this doesn't make you a bad person.

We have the same twenty-four hours in a day that Mother Teresa had! We're capable of overcoming many obstacles; and whatever the challenge or obstacle is … fix it. And, if you can't, then ask yourself, why can't I fix it? What led me to this point of view was adjusting my thought-pattern: "Wait, this isn't me … I'm on Earth to have fun, to laugh, to make other people laugh, and to help others in any way I can."

Being Gifted Is Like
a Baptism
– 21 –

Roslyn Williams Agbata

*Rosyln is a behavioral health counselor and host
of the radio show, Life Matters Today.*

B eing gifted an Intention Stick is like a baptism. When my friend Sandy gifts me an Intention Stick, it turns out to be such a gift in my life, and reminds me of this special experience.

I'm intentional about *Courage*, *Love*, and *Success*, and these are the intentions in my necklace. Most people don't know this: I am the host of *Life Matters Today*. It takes a lot of courage, as an introvert, to stand in front of people on a daily or weekly basis, and talk with them. *Courage* is a word I choose; because each time I get on air, this is an intention that I need for myself. I choose *Love* as well; because love is something that we all need. I want personal love, and I want intimate love with someone, whom I can spend the rest of my life with. *Success* I choose for my business; because I'm an entrepreneur. I want my business to be successful, not only in the world's eyesight, but in God's eyesight.

I chose these three intentions, and received everything I've asked for: I now have a husband, because God has brought love into my life. When I traveled to Africa, and needed the courage to do so, the Intention of *Courage* inside my Intention Stick gifted me the courage I needed. I also had the courage to take a step of faith and build another business. I started my business in the middle of a pandemic; and people asked me, "Why?" This step of faith takes courage. And I do believe, in my heart, that my business will survive and thrive.

Intentions are so powerful. And, to me, the Intention of *Faith* is one of the most powerful. Faith drove success into my life. Faith drove courage into my life. And with faith, I found the love of my life. I've had to be intentional about what I've wanted and to have faith enough to believe it would happen.

This Intention Stick has blessed so many people's lives. I've met many people who wear an Intention Stick, and are talking about how it's blessed them. But this pandemic has a lot of people operating in fear. We're all needing the courage to survive, and keep moving forward.

We can't allow ourselves to be distracted; because how you view the world, and what you think about, will come back to you. This is to say, what you sow, is what you reap. It's like a boomerang. When we think of love and light, when we think of positive words, and gift light and love into other people's lives, we receive light and love in return.

What we say can make things happen; and therefore we have to be careful with our words and intentions. When you're on a higher frequency, and you're giving and receiving, you open yourself up to light, love, and God's creations. I've seen the manifestations of what I believe, and I've seen God's manifestations through so many people who've helped me.

I love and wish for justice – for everyone to be treated equally. And I am setting this intention, so I can share *Love*, *Courage*, and *Faith*. These intentions, in my Intention Stick, may belong to me; but, I would like to gift these intentions to others. I want to gift the Intention of *Love* to someone who may not feel love. So, I'm sowing this into the universe: I'm sowing *Love*, *Courage*, and *Faith* into the universe.

LET GO OF THE GOOD,
TO LET THE GREAT IN
– 22 –

Nick DiFerdinando

Nick is a resilient entrepreneur who has risen from a
troubled teen to a successful businessman: an owner in
a commercial real estate firm, multiple hotel
properties, international investment, and development
project: and is passionate about mentoring,
and inspiring a younger generation of men.

I remember feeling a mental shift; as if I'm letting something go, and letting something else in. The most significant intentions are the one's which align with your life, in this moment, at this present time; so you can thus become aligned with your self, and purpose in life.

The day I receive my Intention Stick, I select the Intentions of *Love*, *Health*, and *Success*. A lot of people expect immediate change after they receive their Intention Stick. This does happen – but for me, life doesn't get dramatically better right after I receive my Intention Stick. As the philosophy suggests, and this is the case with me, "sometimes it gets worse, before it gets better." I have a lot of shifts and changes in my life; but there is also a downward spiral, and I figure out why.

The Intention Stick is powerful for me, and I feel a great shift. Yet, I continue to allow things which aren't serving me – things which make me feel less than about myself and my environment – to stay in my life. All of these shifts have to work for you, not against you. From this, I realize that I'm trying to hold on to old patterns and old relationships which aren't serving me. Because there is only so much room in my life, I can't let anything else in, until I really let go of the past.

I have the intention of wanting the best for everybody. This intention, however, comes across the wrong way. I present myself in a negative way, and begin to notice this; even when I'm trying to help somebody. It presents itself as if I'm judging them, so I've had to adjust this old pattern. Another aspect I've learned is: I have to embrace my bad days. Even the most self-aware people have their best, and worst days; and having a bad day helps me to really focus on the good days. Some of our greatest inventions exist, because of our failures. So, I encourage people to embrace their bad days; because it makes for a better story later.

I begin to make a huge shift when I move from Scottsdale, where I've lived for the past 16 years, to Las Vegas. I sell my home, and decide to get in touch with myself and my intentions; so, I can find a new way to discern my purpose in life. There are many turning points; and, one year, during a birthday dinner, everyone asks questions about my Intention Stick. This is when I feel inspired to place my Intention Stick around my cousin Brian's neck. "This is for you," I say, "and don't ever take it off." The second I clasp the chain around Brian's neck, I have this overwhelming feeling; still, to this day, I cannot describe it ... it's as if something left, and so much more has come into my life for gifting my cousin this Intention Stick.

Brian is usually not receptive to these kinds of experiences; but, in this instance, he is. Brian shares with me, on a phone call, that at certain times, he can feel the energy; and he experiences interactions through the Intention Stick, which makes him feel uplifted. This sense of gifting and wanting the best for people really inspires me and my soul. There is, however, a 'but' to all of this; which is, someone like me doesn't really know how to receive, and I've struggled with this aspect of gifting-and-receiving.

Life is a sequence of stories. My story tends to go into a downward spiral of loneliness, self-sabotage, and depression; all the while, I'm wearing my Intention Stick. It stems from not being able to receive, trying to gift too much, and thus not letting go of the old, so the new can come in.

Some people say, "for the good to come in, you must let go of the bad." However, I don't like to say this. Instead, I like to share with people, whom I mentor and work with: "You have to let go of the good – to let the great in; because there's a fine line between good and great. These things may serve you for the time being. But if you really want to be exceptional and great, and let great things happen, you have to release; because you only have so much room in your life for everything; for love, for business, and for health.

During one of my darkest days, I take off my Intention Stick, because I'm so down, "I don't even want to wear this right now." Previously, I've never taken my Intention Stick off. And, for a period of time, I really wallowed in my own sorrow. Then, one morning, I wake up, and say: "This is the day! This is the day I decide for the shift to happen!" Because, you have to decide to let in all of the great things. And therefore, you have to let go of all of the rest.

So the first thing I do is change my words of intention; and then, I place my Intention Stick on, over my heart. It's as if I haven't worked out in a while, and now I'm working out with great intensity. I feel this substantial difference. It hurts, yet it feels so good. And this is one of those realizations that 'it hurts, yet it feels so good' at the same time. I immediately feel a connection with everyone around me. I can feel the energy. I can feel the support.

I'm able to lean on everyone who's wearing an Intention Stick, and I feel all of the power of their intentions. This has helped me the most – out of anything. Since I decided to make this change, every single one of my intentions – has manifested into reality – has come true. Within weeks of wearing my Intention Stick, a passion project which has been on hold for four years, (as a back-burner vision), has become a reality. It involves mentoring young men, who don't have a gentleman figure to look up to for guidance.

When I wake up in the morning, the Intention Stick is the first thing I think of, and hold – I think about my intentions, and practice gratitude, to start my day. Today, I express gratitude for the opportunity to change someone else's life for the better. And, I will only pick up my phone in the morning to learn something, so as to not distract... I'll practice a language for twenty minutes, journal, and express gratitude; and then, I will embrace the challenges of the day.

I've learned that you don't have to be strong, all the time, for everybody. Although, I still experience dark days, I know now it's how you deal with these dark days, and how you connect with others which really defines your existence and your experience in life.

When I do things for people, and I'm able to help them, it makes me feel good. I've also learned every time someone tries to do something for me, if I don't respect their process to do so, this diminishes the Intention of *Joy* away in their experience. This is an aspect of receiving I am still working on...

KNOWLEDGE CERTAINLY EQUALS ONENESS

– 23 –

Laurie Savoie

Laurie is a loving Mom, author and Speaker bringing Light, Love, and Hope to the World. She is the author of the book, The Ripple Effect.

In 2014, I authored *The Ripple Effect: Invisible Impact of Suicide*. I gift a copy to Marla, and our conversation about life, intention, and the Tree of Life Intention Stick has such an impression on me, I write down the date we met: October 23, 2017. Some time later... Marla shares with me the story of what happens after she placed the book on her kitchen table that night:

"I set your book down, and go to sleep. I'm woken up – as if someone is shaking me, and saying, "Get up, get up, I'm talking to you, get up!" What's going on – who is waking me up? When I wake up, there's nobody there; and the voice continues: Go read my mother's book. Go read my mother's book."

"What's happening here?" I think to myself. So I walk into the kitchen, and there's the book. I open it up, and see this beautiful picture of a young man with the name Garrett; and then, your last name, Savoie. I know this is the voice that said, "get up."

The Ripple Effect is a book I wrote about my son, Garrett, who died by suicide – at nineteen-years-old.

Marla's story continues: "Each time I open the book, and want to proceed to the following page, it flips back to a particular page. So, finally, I re-read the paragraph on this page. It states: you always hated to deal with the "yucky stuff" in life. So, I circle the paragraph, because I know there's a message I need to share with you. The message from Garrett is: it's okay to deal with the "yucky stuff," because there are lessons in it for all of us."

"We need to move on, and not live our lives in the past. However, when we ignore the "yucky stuff," we deny ourselves of the opportunity to learn from these challenges. Furthermore, as we ignore the "yucky stuff," we suppress. And, as we suppress, we don't connect with our truth – with the more honest reality. This is the message I receive to share with you: it's okay, Mom, to deal with the yucky stuff, because we can move on now."

One more auspicious thing happens to Marla the day after Garrett's message: "As I go to our office, I step out of the elevator, onto our floor; and, in front of me, is a directory listing of all the companies located on our floor. The first time, in all the years we have been in this building, I see, in the middle of these listings, *Garrett Development* ... "

When Marla shares the message she receives from Garrett, I know letting go and moving on is one of the hardest lessons in life I will have to learn. My son knows he's loved – there's no question about it. Did he make the wrong choice? Who knows! Was it his choice? I will find out when I greet him in Heaven.

Like Marla, I receive a lot of messages. Garrett is certainly helping me, and is propelling me forward in spirituality – just as he is helping other people.

When I receive my Intention Stick from Marla and Scott, the first intentions which I place inside are *Health* and *Believe*. There's so much energy, and love in the room. The Intention Stick is much more significant than a piece of jewelry. And, since then, I've gifted Intention Sticks to people all over the world.

My youngest daughter is super shy – as her brother used to be. She will be speaking at her school, in front of 200 people. The morning before, she places the Intention of *Oneness* inside her Intention Stick, and I place the Intention of *Knowledge* in mine. She gifts *Knowledge* to everyone in the room, and it has a ripple effect …

Knowledge certainly equals *Oneness*. And, two hundred and one people become a symbol of oneness and knowledge. My daughter receives the confidence to speak, from which her voice flows through her … we all have this divine support available to us, all the time. Our souls know; and our souls also know what we need; this is why I'm always listening.

THE SPOKES OF
THE MEDICINE WHEEL
– 24 –

Dr. Vance Crocker and Dr. Lynn Crocker

Vance, DDS, artist of functional reconstruction,
Divine meditator, Kundalini Yoga Teacher,
Researching the sun, cosmos and all the space
in-between, Husband, Father,
Pappa, Spiritual Warrior.

Lynn, Physician, Healthcare Leader, Vessel of
Compassion ... "through sacred listening
uplifts and opens others to their own healing
and awareness", Integrative Wellness and Design,
Kundalini Yoga teacher, Wife, Mother, Mata,
lover of life ... grateful for every moment.

Lynn:

Trees play an important role in our life. Our property is surrounded by five huge Eucalyptus trees, which are like sen-
tinels and are about protection. The most magnificent one is in
our backyard; her bark is silver, and she has this massive trunk. I

call her Mother Tree. It's truly Mother Tree who inspired me, and gifted me with the message to look for Scott and Marla.

On Mother's Day, I gaze out at Mother Tree, and I'm told, very clearly, that I need to look up the Tree of Life and its meaning. I research the Tree of Life, and the first reference that arrives on my screen is about the Tree of Life Intention Stick. So, I read about Scott and Marla, and think, "I have to meet these people."

Vance:

After Lynn meets Scott and Marla, she becomes really active in sending, and gifting people Intention Sticks.

In the positioning of the Intention Stick over the heartbeat, we actually have neurons in our heart; which is to say, we have a heart brain. At the level of the heart, one of the most electro-magnetically powerful organs of our body, it's almost as if our intentions are transmitted through our heart: a standing wave sort of pulsation, which sends out these intentions.

Every beat of our heart resonates with these intentions. The Intention Stick is a tool that really explains our intentions, and thought-patterns; and this gifts us something to focus on, and transmit from. I wear mine all the time. The specific intentions which I really resonate with are *Kindness, Peace*, and *Compassion*. Anytime someone sees one of the Intention Sticks, they are immediately attracted to it. This attraction sparks the conversation about *Oneness*, again and again.

Everyone's stories become like an affirmation; and we consistently have this conversation about *Oneness*. Everyone relates, and understands it. When you speak the truth, and come from your heart, and your intentions are pure, everyone can relate. I see the correlation about how the Intention Stick is the center plank that brings everyone into this conversation of being *one*: how we come from one source; and now, we're going back to this source.

In each school of thought, whether Kabbalistic, North American Native, Daoist, or Hindu, the spokes of the medicine wheel are coming back together. It's remarkable to see the people who are coming into our lives. They are from every walk of life – from every walk of these schools. This frequency of *Oneness* is almost like sacred geometry; and the spiritual intimacy of this, I cherish a lot.

Lynn:

Like the Tree of Life, we have to be rooted and grounded; so we can manifest our intentions, and consciously be part of the divine. Our true purpose is so much of what the Tree of Life is about... How can we help others, no matter who they are, or where they are? What is their truth? What is their joy? What is their purpose? How do we have compassion, no matter what they're going through?

Clarity exists in everything; because if you didn't know joy, you wouldn't know sadness. If we didn't know light, we wouldn't know darkness. So, it's important we have this perspective, in a conscious way, to help others find what resonates with them.

The Tree of Life Intention Stick is an incredible tool. I carry Intention Sticks with me all the time; because you never know who you're going to meet, and this may be exactly the tool this person needs in their life.

Each time I gift an Intention Stick, I explain, step-by-step, how the blessings and intentions are instilled in this vessel. As a physician, I believe we are vessels, who allow healing energy, in a very pure way, to flow through us. If you can hold this space, without any agenda, then this is when we can shift into a more positive perspective; and thus, this is when miracles occur.

With Covid-19, our hospital staff has been inundated at every moment. I've gifted Intention Sticks to many different patients, and to the entire neuro medical floor staff. One of the nurses starts crying; because I share with her that adults with special needs package the Intention Sticks. Her brother is autistic, and she wants to gift an Intention Stick to him.

In the smaller hospital where I work, many of the ICU nurses are sent to us in south Texas, by the Federal Emergency Management Administration (FEMA), and travel from California and New York, as well as from other states; who have only been taking care of Covid patients. One night, I gift an Intention Stick to one of the nurses, who immediately opens her heart to me.

We are grateful for the jobs we have; because our jobs exist so we can continue to serve our family and friends, our community, and the world in a greater way. This is what we're all here to do in our collective family; which continues to grow, and brings all of these traditions together for understanding and peace; so divisiveness, and polarity, diminishes, until it literally dissolves into love.

TWISTED HAIRS
– 25 –

Mark Johnston

*Mark is an apprentice in the medicine path, a healer, a
sacred storyteller, filmmaker and television
executive with 30 years of storytelling under his belt.*

It's a special night. When I meet Scott and Marla, we're seated
at a table in a hotel ballroom. We're here to celebrate, with
three hundred people, the 98th birthday of Dr. Gladys McGarey
– to honor her journey as a healer, and the light she brings to the
world. Scott leads the entire birthday celebration into a circle, to
hold hands at the end of this evening, for an intentional blessing
ceremony. This is a very special moment. To this day, the energy
from this intentional blessing ceremony remains with me.

The next day, Scott and Marla invite Lindsay and I to receive
our Intention Sticks at their home. They share with us the intention behind their initiative for the global reach of this project
and the impact around the world. Lindsay and I experience our
first moments together; connecting with how we can live a life of
intention. This experience is deeply special; because Scott and
Marla, the two souls who created this beautiful piece with divine
guidance, gift each of us an Intention Stick.

Scott asks if Linsday and I would like to participate in a meditation-based intention ceremony; where the person who gifts the Intention Stick to you, in this case, Scott, selects an intention for you; and, as you open your Intention Stick thirty days later, you reflect on this intention. In addition to this meditation-based intention ceremony, Lindsay and I also select our own intentions to place inside our Intention Stick. The gift of intention, when someone special to you selects a positive intention for you to wear over your heart, really speaks to me.

Lindsay also selects an intention for me; and I discover, one month later, that the intention is *Be, Let It Be*. She feels this intention is important for my journey. So, I respect the process of surrendering to *Be, Let it Be*. As I learn this idea of letting go of control, and thus surrendering, I develop the faith and trust that each of us are being guided on a daily basis; this leads me to the idea of "carrying rocks" – as affirmed within the medicine path. The idea of "carrying rocks" is to have a life where one releases and stops holding onto these rocks, and thus lets go – to let it be. How light our journey will be – if we walk with the Intention of *Be, Let It Be*.

It's an amazing interaction and experience to ask the people closest to you to participate in this process; which – as you open your Intention Stick thirty days later – you connect with the intention someone gifts and selects for you. Then, you reflect on the previous month and see the moments where you connect the dots with this intention; and think, "I remember this experience at work. I remember feeling frustrated and being challenged. At this moment, I recall being able to *Be, Let It Be*." Things move gracefully as I wear this intention. I recall experiencing these moments – a few times – when the light turns on!

Lindsay's intention for me has come to fruition. This significant aspect of the gift of intention appears within my first steps and experiences as I wear my intentions over my heart. This is the beginning of my journey as a recipient of the Intention Stick. I've become someone who loves to share this gift with others. Because of this personal impact, it has helped me to understand the value and weight of the work Scott and Marla aspire to; and this has really inspired me to reach out to others, so they can live a life of intention.

The Intention of *Trust* is a very common thread and theme among friends I've gifted Intention Sticks to; because for whatever reason, we've been conditioned, or we simply try, to control everything in our lives. It seems when we are aware there is a greater choreography at play – which is, by far, much larger than us – if we can trust in this vision and direction, then there's a stronger, clearer reason to co-create with others on a daily basis.

The light that grows in people who wear the Intention Stick is truly a gift; because it inspires us to do better work, and to help others. The Intention Stick impacts the people who wear them, every single day. I've seen the tribe grow, the ripple effect of this journey, and the beauty that continues to arise from the gift of the Intention Stick.

There is a Native tradition known as "twisted hairs." As the Native person moves away from their own tribe, to learn the beauty and wisdom of other Native tribes, they bring this beauty and wisdom back to their own culture and environment; to thus improve the overall life and dynamic of their own inner circle. These Natives are known as "twisted hairs."

So many people whom I've interacted with have different backgrounds, and belief systems. The Intention Stick is a universal symbol that encourages us to ground into the idea of living with intention. It also reminds us that we are interconnected and interdependent. Yet, we are all the same ... the rest is just packaging.

With a gift of this nature, by gifting someone this beautiful piece, their worthiness comes forward; because they are honored, thought of, and graced with a sacred piece, by divine design, to wear over their heart each day. The Intention Stick encourages, supports, and reminds us to live in our highest way. We are here on Earth, to live a life of intention; from which we can create a better life for ourselves.

This invisible impact we have in our hands, as we gift an Intention Stick to someone, energetically comes back and lifts us up. I sit in grace, gratitude, humility, and love knowing that the Intention Stick I gifted has helped them move onward in their life and journey. The Intention Stick, for me, in a sense, is like the "twisted hairs"; because this has improved my life, and has improved the beauty and wisdom in my life.

I continue to gift the Intention Stick to friends and family in my inner circle, so they can learn different ways to be intentional with themselves and their tribes – their family and friends – to live a life of intention.

FEMIFEST AND LIVING
INTO THE LIGHT
– 26 –

Dr. Gladys McGarey and Rose Winters

*Dr. Gladys is a visionary whose pioneering
accomplishments include being the Mother of
Holistic Medicine, the first to bring acupuncture to
this country, advocating for Dads in the delivery
room, teaching safer birthing practices to women
in war -torn rural Afghanistan, and the list goes on.
She received her first literary contract at age 100!*

*Rose has more than 30 years of experience
in all facets of the non-profit arena. She has
served more than 10 years as the CEO of
the Foundation For Living Medicine.*

Dr. Gladys McGarey:

My Intention Stick contains the word *Gratitude*. When my oldest daughter and I are having a lecture, one of the audience members approaches me; "Dr. Gladys, what is your secret?"

I guess she's referring to my long life. I'm trying to come up with something cute and profound as a response; and I can't come up with anything. I receive an elbow – a nudge – from my daughter; "Mom, you do too know, you dwell in gratitude." This is true. I am so grateful for everything that's happened. The good times and the hard times, the illnesses and the wellness. I am grateful for my amazing life, and the amazing people who are shining a light on what needs to be done in this world. I am one hundred years old, and I am so honored and happy to be alive right now.

When I was two years old, back in India, where my parents were medical missionaries, I discovered that I wasn't going to become a doctor. Instead, I discovered that I already was one.

Over a lifetime, I've come to do this medical work, and the work is living life; which is why we call our foundation, "The Foundation for Living Medicine." We've spent eons of time working with killing disease, or killing this or that. It's been a war against disease. I've discovered this has its place and time. There are times when you have to go to war, but that's not the purpose of life. Life has to do with living. If we can focus our intention, and energy on living into the light, then there is something to live for.

In the process of these years of evolving my life, and learning the lessons I've had to learn, I understand that we need to have places on this Earth where people can work with themselves, and contact physicians, as they evolve their life purpose. We all need each other. We don't have five races. We have one race. It's the human race.

As I've walked this path, I've become aware that "The Foundation for Living Medicine" has five L's. The first L is (Life). The second L is (Love). Life by itself is like a seed on the ground. It's full of the energy that is life, but can't do anything until love, which is the activating God spark, activates it. Love activates life. Then, the two – love and life – can work together, so life starts. The whole process of life itself, on this Earth dimension, has the positive and the negative; which have to come together.

The third L is (Laughter): Laughter without love is cruel, cold, and mean. But laughter with love is happiness and joy. You can live in happiness. And this is what we wish, and pray for. The fourth L is (Labor). Labor without love is drudgery, hard, and mean. It wears you out, and it takes an awful lot of energy. But labor with love is bliss. It's why you sing. It's what encourages the painter to paint. The fifth L is (Listening). Listening without love is an empty sound. But listening with love is understanding.

Someone hears me talk about the five L's, and they ask, "But what about gratitude? What about hope? What about compassion?" I say, "Those are the building blocks with which you build on the foundation for living medicine." The whole field of medicine, for me, has never had a foundation until these five L's. This is the foundation which we are now working with; to create not only a loving birth center, but a village for living medicine. It has to manifest on this Earth. Though, now, I use another word that has entered my vocabulary. It's the word Femifest.

Femifesting is an energy that is different. Manifesting is climbing Jacob's Ladder. Femifesting is on a spiral instead of a stepping stone. You can be up on the fifth level when femifesting, and look down and know what's going on at other levels. I had a dream that laid this whole thing out, and I think that's what is coming together now. If we bring the male energy and female energy together, we can begin to understand compassion and understand loving.

I couldn't have arrived halfway on this path, if it hadn't been for Rose, who entered my life – I don't know how long ago. And, through thick and thin, up and down, Rose is still here.

Rose:

During the AIDS epidemic, I created an AIDS organization, and that was my introduction to the health care world. Through my work with AIDS patients, I met Dr. Elisabeth Kubler Ross, the psychiatrist who pioneered grief counseling, and she became a wonderful friend. She suggested that I contact Dr. Gladys McGarey on a project I wanted to create specifically for children.

The courage and the inner knowing that Dr. Gladys has held – and her vision – is so huge that it encompasses the entire world. I have been working with her on bringing into reality her vision for a village of Living Medicine, adopted from the definition that the Native American people use for medicine. It's life. This is a village for life, and it isn't just for people who have a medical diagnosis of some form. It's a place to be born again, in a sense, to your higher self. The village concept is built on humanity, it's built on harmony, and it's built on beauty. It's going to be such a landscape that the moment your foot touches the ground, a healing and a different vibrational energy will flow through you, leading to the healing that you seek.

Dr. Gladys and I, along with Marla and Scott, share a dream for the future of our children; we are here to soften the paths to gift our children the real meaning of life. This is why, to us, the Intention Stick isn't a piece of jewelry. When we wear the Intention Stick, we are wearing the biggest aspect of ourselves, and our biggest dream for the world, no matter how we intend that vision to be.

WE'RE ALWAYS BEING GUIDED
– 27 –

Nicole Myden

Nicole is Founder of The PR Concierge, which helps small businesses share their purposes and missions in the media. She relocated from Los Angeles to Scottsdale and discovered the Tree of Life Movement her first year living in Arizona.

A few months after moving from Los Angeles to Scottsdale for a new design of life, I meet a Rabbi who's now a wonderful friend. I share with him how I want to connect, both soulfully and energetically, with like-minded people, but I haven't found them here, yet.

"I have the perfect couple for you to meet," the Rabbi says.

Within a few days, I have a groundbreaking meeting with Scott and Marla. It's like a spiritual lovefest. They gift an Intention Stick to me, and I know that I'm aligning with people who are on the same soul mission. The Intention Stick comes into my life at such a divine time. It feels so meaningful to receive its healing-love and -light, and the added layer of protection it provides.

I'm so excited to introduce new people to Marla and Scott, and the Tree of Life Movement. I've been intentional when I bring people to their office – when I know they need something meaningful; to remind them that they are loved and supported, and that they are not alone.

Every person I bring with me, instantly, connects with Marla and Scott and their mission; and, immediately, they open up their hearts and become ambassadors for the Tree of Life Movement. People understand it – when they hear the story of the Intention Stick and the Tree of Life Movement. I've seen this firsthand; you see the lightbulb turn on. It has such a beautiful impact.

I've experienced miracles, and I've seen many people around me experience miracles. I've seen the power of what's going on here – the physical healing. The key is that we're all meeting each other at a time when we're open to receive the miracle of intention.

I periodically change the words inside my Intention Stick, and I have the Intentions of *Health*, *Love*, and *Light*. The Intention of *Health* is really important; yet, my health hasn't always been the best. It's been a challenging time during the pandemic. I live alone, I run a business, and I'm trying to keep everything afloat.

I'm a part of the generation who went to college, and went to Corporate America, in order to check this off the list. The world defined success for me before I defined it for myself; if I didn't have a certain car, if I didn't marry a certain person, or if I didn't belong to a country club. This is why I felt guided to move to Arizona: to define happiness and success for myself. And, I'm happier than I've ever been.

Through the power of the Intention Stick, I've realized that I must gift myself with grace and love, and therefore not beat myself up. I feel an incredible shift in my life – and in my body – every day. I feel as if I am releasing energy which no longer serves me. I've learned to relinquish control and enjoy the ride; to enjoy the journey. It's scary to let go and trust. But if your soul can master this one life lesson – to let go and trust – imagine how much more joyful we could be in our interactions with our family, friends, and colleagues. Because what's for you, will find you, we just have to trust that we're always being guided.

I'm excited for the future; that it will bring people together at a pivotal time. We're set free to just be ourselves, and float the overarching message; which is detachment from the outcome. I've finally learned to put myself out there. And if it doesn't work out, it's okay; because, if what you want does not work out, it's simply because you're being protected.

LEAP OF FAITH

– 28 –

Katie Kyleen Sabbaghian

Katie is a spiritual psychologist, international teacher, and founder of Gateway Healing.

I t's been a long time since I've had a mystical experience. I believe life is more meaningful with these paranormal, or supernatural, experiences which connect with you. The mystical experience I receive from the moment Marla and Scott place an Intention Stick around my neck is so incredible, I have tears in my eyes.

"I want to share this experience with everyone else," I remember thinking. "How can I do this? How can I share this with everyone else – the feeling I just felt? How can I share this with my friends, and with my own community?"

Even in the moment you make the decision to wear this spiritual tool, you feel the energy starting to work. For anyone who says the Intention Stick is just a piece of jewelry, there's more to understand…

At our first event, where I introduce Marla and Scott to my own community, there are more than sixty people. I feel very nervous; because I want my students and friends to feel this energy. The question I consider is: "Are they going to feel it in the same way that I do?" Following Scott and Marla's story, and our guided meditation, we all stand up and join hands in a circle. The students share that they can feel this current of energy – I am overjoyed.

I have two stories which I'm inspired to share about the Intention Stick: While in the Middle East, in Dubai, I'm leading classes, teaching, and holding private sessions. In the midst of being in Dubai, this lady, who would like a private session, approaches me. She inquires for a spiritual reading – yet, my gut clearly tells me that she needs an inner healing; which is to say, she needs to shift something within herself.

She has a son with Down Syndrome. And, for the previous year, she has been visiting many different healers, trying to find a way to heal her son. This is emphasized to the point where she almost seems obsessed with her mission. I recall tuning in with her – the way she thinks, breathes, lives, acts, and exists; and as clear as day, I see this image of her in a past life.

From this image of her in a past life, I sense that she's been this free woman, doing whatever she wants in the world. She's had many lives thinking of self, and not in service of anyone else. This is the message I receive: "Your child is actually a gift for you – to have selfless love in this lifetime; and to learn what it is to care for someone else. This is your soul contract. Your son isn't going to heal. It's actually meant to be this way."

When I share this message with her, I receive a resistant response – a negative reaction. Yet, I trust not to back down. I try to share this message in a different light; in any way I try to share this with her, she's not open to hearing it.

Over the course of this next week, I continue to meet with other people. This woman continues to send messages via text to me, questioning the message I've shared. After a week, when it's nearly time for me to leave Dubai, I consider meeting with her again. As I'm pondering this question, whether or not I should meet with her? – I glance over at my luggage; and there is an Intention Stick. My last one. As a way to help her move past this, (what she's holding onto), I gift my Intention to her…

The next day, when we meet, I share the story of the Intention Stick. I read the list of intentions to her, and she can't decide which intentions to choose. She asks me to select the intentions for her. The intention which I sense she needs is *Be, Let It Be*. I select the Intention of *Be, Let It Be* inside her Intention Stick. As I place the Intention Stick around her neck, she breaks down in tears. She cries in heaves, all the way to her heart. When she settles downs, I ask her:

"What are you feeling?"

"I think, for the first time, I know my true purpose," she says.

"What is your true purpose?" I ask.

"My purpose is to be the best mother I can be," she says.

In this moment, the acceptance she needs has come from the gift of the intention: *Be, Let It Be*.

This is what I love about the Intention Stick. It's a vessel for something much higher to come through us. It's a conduit, a channel, an instrument. When we place the Intention Stick over our heart, we're in alignment with the desire of our soul. When we select and wear our intentions, we're saying, "God, this is what is most sacred to me." The Intention Stick brings the woman in Dubai a way to come into alignment with her intentions and her true purpose.

The story I'm also inspired to share with you happens during this same trip in Dubai. Before traveling to Dubai, I pick up several Intention Sticks from Marla. The morning I meet with Marla, she shares with me that she's had a vision of this girl in Africa who's part of an orphanage. Marla feels that she has to find her, and gift her an Intention Stick. It happens to be the case, from Dubai, I'm traveling to Africa. Marla, Scott, and I hold an Intention Stick, and we say an intentional blessing ceremony for this girl.

"We know you're going to find this little girl," Marla says to me; "and we know you'll know who this belongs to when you see her."

Nearly two-thirds of the way into my trip in Africa, my hosts bring me to an orphanage. As I'm here, I'm searching in all the kid's eyes. "Which one are you?" I consider; however, the lady who's hosting me shares: "Please don't. Because, if you give this to one girl, what will happen is, in the night, someone will come and take it off her neck, and then sell it. Anything that is shiny, or brand new, gets taken from them, and sold." I feel so heartbroken, because I made this commitment.

A few days pass, and I see a young girl across the street. I'm drawn to her. When I meet her, she shares with me how both of her parents are gone, and she's been left to raise her three siblings, alone; barely making it on her own, she's been going through a rough time, both emotionally and financially. I know, in my heart, this is the girl. So, I say the blessings of intention, and gift the Intention Stick to this young girl. She's so shy, so sweet, and humble. The gift brings such a big smile to her face. I capture a photo of her as she's smiling and wearing her Intention Stick, so I can share this moment.

I remember thinking: "There's my girl."

When I return to Arizona, and share this story with Scott and Marla, they are inspired. They begin researching how they can create an Intention Stick that's not shiny, and thus will not attract unwanted and unwarranted attention; and, therefore, will not place any child in a harmful situation. Scott has this vision of the Intention Stick, which is a pure white vessel, to represent the soul of each child; which leads Scott and Marla to their inspiration and their vision of the Tree of Life Movement Foundation.

Lastly, I have one more miracle story to share. This is from another event, for my community, where Scott and Marla participate. Before this event, I receive a message from a lady via text: "Hi Katie, you don't know who I am, but I would really like to come to this event, but I can't afford it. Is there any chance I can come and maybe pay you later when I find a job?" She continues to explain how she's been out of a job for an entire year, and only has one month of savings to pay for her rent.

"Yes, of course, you can attend and join us; please, don't worry about paying."

She attends the event, and hears Scott and Marla share their story. She's so connected with their message that she decides to take some of her rent money, and purchase an Intention Stick. Knowing that she won't have enough money for rent, she takes this leap of faith.

"Katie, I have a confession to make," she shares with me the next day. "I purchased an Intention Stick, because I felt so called to do it. And I selected two intentions to go inside. But I am stuck on the third intention. Which one should I choose?" My first thought is, she should select the Intention of *Faith*; because faith is knowing that God will deliver, even though we don't have tangible proof of this yet. It's walking blindly, knowing that it will come. So, this beautiful soul chooses *Faith* as her third intention.

After she chooses her intentions, she brings her child to a school event. She walks in with her son, they enter the school elevator, and before the door closes, another Mom hastily runs into the elevator with her daughter. The mom is having a loud conversation via her phone. She's frustrated, and complaining about a work position which hasn't been filled yet. The position is very specialized: a forensic analyst. "I am actually looking for that position," the lady says to the woman, when they both get out of the elevator. "I can send you my resume from my phone."

She has taken this leap of faith, receives an Intention Stick, selects the Intention of *Faith*, and she is gifted the forensic analyst position. I hear miraculous stories like this surrounding the Intention Stick all of the time!

An Inspiring Sign of Hope
– 29 –

Pat and Duffy McMahon

*Pat hosts The God Show on radio and Duffy is a
doctor in human sexuality who does
the podcast, Life Happens*

Duffy:

When I meet Scott and Marla, I'm hosting a podcast, *Life Happens*. He shares the story of the Intention Stick, the symbolic meaning of the Tree of Life, and the purpose of sacred numbers; all of which I'm interested in and love. I ask for an Intention Stick, and Scott gifts one to me.

I share with my husband Pat – that I met the most fascinating person who created – the Intention Stick, and the twenty-two words of intention that can go inside. It makes sense to me that the powerful words you wear close to your heart can have a major impact on your life.

The Intention Stick reminds me on a daily basis that I have love, I have intention, I have mindfulness, and all of the things that help keep me on track; it's a reminder when I'm feeling sorry for myself. I can hold my Intention Stick and feel a sense of purpose. The Intentions of *Believe*, *Blessed*, *Oneness*, and *Happiness* are so important for us as human beings; because how you speak and interact with these intentions means so much.

The Intention Stick is so meaningful for me, and for everyone else I've gifted one to…I gift an Intention Stick to our friend's son, who's graduating from college, as a graduation present. "Before you open it, I just want to tell you a little story." So, I share with him about Marla and Scott, the symbolic meaning of the Tree of Life, and what an Intention Stick supports and encourages. His eyes well up with tears. "Duffy, you have no idea. My girlfriend and I were going out to look for something I could wear around my neck – to have it close to my heart. I didn't know what it was going to be – and this is it!" he emphasizes.

We really need the Intention Stick gifted globally, because the world has been pulled apart. And the more we are pulled apart, the more confusing and sad it becomes, when people seem lost and don't know what to do. And for this: An Intention Stick is a grounding and an inspiring sign of hope. When it comes to the Tree of Life, we are all a part of this tree; which is to say, we are all one. Why should it matter which culture, color, nationality, or gender you are? We are all human beings, trying to live and learn as much as we possibly can … and we share a universal symbol with the Tree of Life, and the Intention Stick.

Pat:

After meeting Scott and Marla, and receiving my own Intention Stick, I invite them as guests on my radio show, *The God Show*, about spirituality. Our conversation entails the Tree of Life Movement and the Intention Stick. Rosemary, my producer for twenty years, is a former nun. She left the convent to become a mom. She's crying through most of the hour-long interview with Scott and Marla. Over the years, the guests on our show have been people from every background. I have never seen Rosemary's heart and soul so touched by one of the guests on my show. After

Scott and Marla's appearance, Rosemary emphasizes to me that she will always remember Scott and Marla; because they aren't trying to direct people to a specific philosophy or faith.

Years ago, Mother Teresa appears as a guest on my show. This is during the time when she's opening a convent in Phoenix with three sisters from Calcutta – to help take care of the needy. I ask her, while we're on the air, what she needs. Usually, when it comes to religious folks, it has something to do with a collection box; because they have bills to pay as well. But, instead, Mother Teresa suggests, "Share with your audience that tomorrow morning, when they wake up, they should find someone who has no one, and love them." This is a simple, yet powerful message. What a thrill it would've been to gift Mother Teresa with an Intention Stick.

Another guest who appears on my show is the Dalai Lama. What a thrill it would've been to gift the Dalai Lama with an Intention Stick. Both of them – Mother Teresa and the Dalai Lama – would have understood the Intention Stick with very little need for explanation. There is no faith which can fail to find deep meaning in the Intention Stick.

Reset My Intentions
– 30 –

Lee Mudro

Lee is Founder and Owner of Lee Mudro LLC, certified emotion code and body code practitioner who is holistically healing breast cancer by energy work, supplements and organic eating.

As soon as I hear Scott and Marla, I know there's a connection between us, and I'm compelled to receive one of these Intention Sticks. I'm with a group of people, and we're listening to Scott and Marla. When I share my story, and ask them which words I should place inside the Intention Stick, they share with me and suggest: *Success, Be, Let It Be,* and *Trust.*

I attend a seminar about energy healing the following weekend. And, instantly, I know this is what I need to do; so, I sign up for courses to learn how to be an energy healer. Now, I've been doing this work for over two years. It seems when you lose your job – which is the case with me, that morning, right before I meet Scott and Marla – the Universe is guiding you to a new opportunity. You just have to go look for it!

I gift so many Intention Sticks to my family and friends. And, I really think the Intention Stick has helped shift their perspective; that this has helped create and strengthen a positive difference in their life.

My first step forward, when I'm diagnosed with breast cancer, is to speak with Scott and Marla. "Which intentions should I place in my Intention Stick?", since I want to be intentional with the intentions I need to become healthy. Scott and Marla suggest the Intentions of *Trust*, *Happiness*, *Health*, and *Oneness*.

The cancer is located in my right breast. From a spiritual point of view, the right breast symbolizes the masculine-energy. I've been married several times, so I know where the cancer stems from; and to have a disease as serious as cancer, I must be holding on to something. For me, it also connects with negative experiences, which derive from my childhood.

We carry so many negative experiences, thoughts, and patterns from our childhood, which are saturated and rooted deeply within us. This seems to be the extent to how I can reach these experiences, thoughts, and patterns; through something as substantial as cancer. We all seem to suffer – or at least most of us do – from negative experiences which we suppress from our childhood. These experiences can create negative energy blocks within the body – sort of like a clogged pipe. It's only later in life when it emerges and shows up as a disease, an illness, or pain.

Cancer is a negative energy, a negative thing, which I need to release, so my body and mind can heal itself. I have an invasive type of cancer. It's an aggressive cancer, but not the most extreme case of breast cancer. I have five aunts in my family who've had breast cancer. They all had mastectomies, and didn't die from their cancer. So, whichever way this journey goes, I have to consider alternative ways in order to become healthy. So, I choose a natural, holistic path to healing. I know when I overcome this challenge, it will change and shift my perspective, and the way I move forward, in positive ways. And thus, I have to reset my intentions in order to overcome this challenge.

I select the Intention of *Trust* for my Intention Stick, because I must trust my own intuitive sense and knowing; such that I will be able to make the right decision based on what I'm feeling, and what I'm hearing. The words "radiation" and "chemo" for cancer give me such a stomachache when I hear it; and I cannot willingly put these poisons inside my body. Maybe it works for other people, simply because they believe this medicine will save them. However, for me, I don't think it will work, because I don't believe in it. So, I trust that I am going to heal myself in a way that feels right – the appropriate way for me.

It's good to know that when this is over, I'm not going to bring anything like this illness into my life again. This has been a big wake-up call. But it's going to be finished. I'm going to have the Intention of *Health*. And, no matter what happens, I am going to be happy. This is a time to be around family – who I'm very close to – who make me happy. This is why I also choose the Intention of *Happiness*.

This is one of the best years I've had in a very long time; so it's kind of shocking that cancer emerges in my life. These things creep up, and really show that there's something within you to focus and work on. The fourth intention I have inside my Intention Stick is *Oneness*. Everyone within my family, and my friends constantly say prayers for me. And I totally believe prayers can help heal anything. I've seen miracles so many times. And I have a prayer group. So far, we're all doing very well.

I continue to share the Tree of Life Movement and the Intention Stick with my friends, family, and with everyone whom I meet. The Intention Stick is the best thing you can gift to anyone. So, choose an intention you want to have for yourself, or for somebody else, because these intentions really work. We are all one. And the Intention Stick helps us to unify the world.

The greatest example, I know, which demonstrates this philosophy is with two eggs: a brown egg and a white egg. If you open both of these eggs up, what's inside? Exactly the same thing. In this example, we have to remember: It doesn't matter what the outside shell looks like – we are all one!

SERENDIPITIES AND THE POWER OF INTENTION
– 31 –

Dr. Steve Hruby and Dray Carson-Hruby

*Steve is a happy father and Founder of the pain relief
and anti-aging clinic, Kaizen Progressive Health,
and a co-founder of SuperHuman supplement line
and a performance and longevity coach. Dray is a
proud Momma, Corporate Development Consultant
and the owner of the healthy Whole Plant Matters
skin and supplement line, and Co-Founder (with
her daughter) of Bag of Change, supporting kids
freed from human trafficking in the U.S.*

Dray:

The Intention Stick creates a sense of unity; a sense of connection to people we may not even know ... wherever I am, I feel an immediate connection to someone who's wearing an Intention Stick. Yet, this connection is not from knowing this person. It's a connection from the heart, from our intentions ... which can also be for other people, including our family and beyond ...

I'm introduced to Scott and Marla, through a mutual friend. This is during a really challenging time in my life. When I receive my Intention Stick, I listen to my inner voice to guide me to the right intentions. When I arrive home, I show my husband Steve...

Steve:

Intention has been a powerful tool for me. When I meet Dray, I'm listening to one of Dr. Wayne Dyer's videos on the power of intention. I really connect with this philosophy; and, at this point in my life, I'm going through this horrible incident, or what seems to be a horrible incident; and, yet, this turns out to be the biggest gift...

So, I set all of these positive intentions, not just for myself, but also for my children and all the people in my life; and from this moment onward, beautiful things – all of these serendipities – start to happen in my life. And one of the biggest moments is when I meet Dray.

In addition, all of the stars appear to align when I realize Travis, who's one of my staff members, has been introduced to Scott and Marla and the Intention Stick. These serendipities have been a sign and message, to emphasize that this is the right path for me, as I move forward.

We are all having the same kind of human experience; yet, at the same time, we have different parts to play in the overall script of life. Ultimately, we seek connection with one another; and is why the powerful universal message of the Intention Stick – and one of the words of intention – is *Oneness*.

Dray:

The present I gift to people, who I feel a deep, spiritual soul connection with, is the Intention Stick. "You have no idea how perfect this timing was for me," they say. As with many veterans, who have gone through many deployments, you can see it in their eyes. My cousin is a retired veteran, who was deployed many times, and I gifted the Intention Stick to him. You this see at a soul level; because, whether they're religious or not, or whether they appreciate rituals or not, they believe in intention and a higher power to guide them.

The experience that occurs when I choose two intentions, ask Scott to select the third intention for me, and Scott clasps the necklace on me, is I feel as if I can breathe easier. And, before I open my Intention Stick, to see the third intention, Scott asks me to be patient; to wait thirty days ...

When I open my Intention Stick thirty days later, to see which intention Scott placed inside, the intention is *Light*. I previously glanced over this; because I thought this intention seems similar to when people suggest, "seeing the light."

What I experience that day, when Scott places the Intention Stick over my heart, is a lightness in my chest. This Intention of *Light* shows me how someone else's intention (how a close friend's or family member's intention) for you can be physically, emotionally, and spiritually manifested.

NOTE TO READER
FROM SCOTT AND MARLA

* * *

Scott:

D ray arrives at my office, and is inspired to purchase Intention Sticks for Christmas, as gifts for her friends and family. This is the first time she learns about the Silicon Intention Stick. I share the meaning and story that the Silicon Intention Stick is for children who are at-risk.

Alongside her daughter Sasha, Dray founded *Bags of Change*. From which they raise monies, for items they purchase, to create gift bags for the children and young adults who have been recused from sex trafficking; at the Dream Center in Phoenix, as gifts to support their physical, emotional, or spiritual change.

Yet, Dray emphasizes that she feels there's "a spiritual component" that's missing; that she gifts these bags, and afterwards, still feels as if there's something else to attend to ... to provide additional support for these children and young adults.

After sharing the story of the Silicon Intention Stick, Dray and I call Marla. Marla shares the story of her vision (the dream) that she has of a young girl who lives in a village in Africa; whom, when our dear friend Katie visits Kenya, connects with a young girl, and gifts her with an Intention Stick (Chapter

28). Marla also shares the philosophy – the point of view – that children are the seeds of our future; and it is our obligation and responsibility to encourage and help our children grow in every way possible – as to live a life of intention (Chapter 42).

Marla:

I share with Dray the significance of what she's doing with her daughter Sasha, and the importance to help support one another in a spiritual way; to help support young adults and children connect with a positive state of awareness, with a positive sense of self, that they are loved, that they can will their dreams into fruition; and, ultimately, there is someone who believes in them, so they feel encouraged to believe in themselves.

As I share this message with Dray, she's inspired to purchase fifty-four Silicon Intention Sticks. Dray feels this is the spiritual component, and leads all of us, including Sasha, to the Dream Center in Phoenix; to gift the Silicon Intention Sticks to the children and young adults who have been rescued; and, in a circle, we hold hands with the children for an intention blessing ceremony; from which they select their intentions to wear around their heart.

We believe that after children and young adults receive the essentials, the nutrients to survive and live a healthy life, we cannot merely walk away; because there are the spiritual components and aspects to attend to; to feel encouraged, inspired, and loved.

Because there is mental, emotional, and physical health to attend to, we also emphasize that there's always another step we can do for spiritual health; to help in meaningful ways where this will encourage, impel, and compel children, where they will feel encouraged, impelled, and compelled to move forward, as to grow and strengthen their self from within.

THE INTENTION OF
KNOWLEDGE

* * *

Marla:

As I share my story and recollection – the previous note to reader about Dray – this reminds me of the time Scott and I are in LA, when we meet a dear friend of ours for lunch ... we share, and gift him with the Intention Stick.

Before we leave for LA, I'm inspired to change my intention. Yet, I think to myself, "it's fine, I'll leave it be ... " because we're already in the car and I don't have the intentions with me. At first, I feel anxious about this; because, for some reason, I feel impelled to change my intention ...

We arrive in LA. And, as we're at lunch, Mike is tapping his foot. He's going to a meeting after lunch and will be pitching a new TV series; and seems nervous about how this meeting will go ...

Because we didn't have the words of intention for Mike to place inside, I encourage Mike to share and visualize the intention he's inspired by; the intention he's inspired to arrive with ...

I recall asking Mike, "if you can choose any intention to place inside, which intention do you need?"

"Knowledge," Mike affirms.

"You're never going to believe this," I say, as I unclasp my Intention Stick and take out the only intention I have inside … (there's a reason I didn't change my intention before going to lunch).

And so, Mike places the Intention of *Knowledge* inside his Intention Stick. And, after lunch, following Mike's meeting, he sends us a message; about how the meeting went … it was amazing; incredible, Mike emphasizes.

The intention gifts, and guides Mike with the knowledge he asks for and is inspired by.

A Constant and Physical Reminder

– 32 –

Jeffrey Winer

*Jeffrey is a marketing professional with
25 years of experience in the bio-pharmaceutical
industry. His life changed and he started on a
path of enlightenment on Feb. 19, 2008, when he
donated his kidney to his best friend's father.*

While attending my company's national business meeting at a resort in Scottsdale, Arizona, several coworkers and I nearly walk by a jewelry store after breakfast. As we walk inside, my attention is directed to a collection of necklaces in a display – and, at first glance, I think they're mezuzahs.

When I ask the store manager, she shares, "they're not mezuzahs, these are Intention Sticks." She briefly explains the story and meaning behind the Intention Stick, and it's wonderful to learn what they are; because I'm searching for a number of gifts, one of which is for a Bat Mitzvah.

Because I purchase ten Intention Sticks, the store manager informs Scott; from which he sends me a text message, asking if we can meet.

The next day, I have a long break in between my company's business meetings; so I walk over to the jewelry store…

Scott is there, with his wife, Marla, saying goodbye to a customer.

While in conversation with Scott and Marla, Marla asks, "I recognize your accent… where are you from?"

"I'm from Akron, Ohio," I reply.

"Do you know my great uncle, Lou Stile?" Marla asks.

My jaw hits the floor, and I drop the bags I'm carrying; "you mean, my uncle?!"

All three of us are in a state of amazement, from this pleasantly unexpected (double emphasis of a) surprise.

It's divinely guided how we are connected. The three of us stand in the middle of the boutique. We hold hands, say intentional blessings for my Intention Stick, and the Intention Sticks I'm going to gift.

I choose the Intention of *Success*. Marla and Scott select the other two, (the Intentions of *Trust* and *Inspire*), and ask me not to look at the intentions for thirty days.

Since then, placing my Intention Stick on each morning is a constant and physical reminder to be mindful. There have been times when I lose my temper, or become aggravated at something or someone; and, all of a sudden, I'll feel the Intention Stick… it brings me back, and reminds me to be mindful.

Most often, when people think of the Intention of *Success*, they immediately consider the material means and monetary value; looking to the external aspects in life, rather than the internal, and spiritual point of view. As for me, the word *Success* in my Intention Stick doesn't necessarily relate to money. It can relate to success in my relationships, success for love, and, in its most general sense, success within each aspect of life.

When I gift Intention Sticks to friends and family, I share the story and message of what it means to me. And, just as Marla and Scott did for me, I select two intentions for them. Then, I ask them to choose a third intention; to be patient and wait thirty days before opening it up.

Thirty days later, I'll ask, once they've looked inside, "what do these intentions mean to you?" I encourage them to carry this message they've received with them, thereafter, as they move forward, from one moment to the next...

IT'S LIKE WEARING A
LIFE JACKET
– 33 –

Sean Erick

*Sean went from eating "Meals on Wheels," as a
kid, to eating in every continent, sans Antarctica,
by performing his trumpet with some of the
world's greatest performers all over the planet.
He has donated funds to serve over 24k in meals
to Americans in need last year alone, making him
someone called a self-proclaimed "civilionaire."*

I have been fortunate to make a successful career out of playing
music. Nobody knows who I am, but I've played with many of
the world's most renowned musical artists. It's been a beautiful
ride. And I feel as if my life reflects *The Lord of the Rings* trilogy.

While in the fourth grade, I'm introduced to my instrument:
the trumpet.

"You can either go make noise in the gym every Tuesday,
or you can sit somewhere and read quietly," they say. And, of
course, I want to make noise. My upbringing is low income,
section 8 housing, Meals on Wheels. But it's a racially diverse

community with all sorts of music and other influences. I have a bunch of teachers throwing me out of class, saying; I will never amount to anything. It takes very special, warm, big-hearted people to see through the outer layer of chaos: a defense which I created for myself…

It's through my friend Brian – and a series of connections and timing of events – I'm connected with Scott and Marla.

When I first receive my Intention Stick, I select the Intentions of *Love* and *Light*. Then, Brian selects a third word for me: *Gratitude*. I'm kind of taken aback by this; because it makes me feel slightly uncomfortable. "Do you think I'm not grateful? What do you mean by gratitude?" I ask Brian – who's a good friend; he sees an intention, for me, which makes a lot of sense.

Over time, as I wear this Intention Stick, I've become more familiar with how to be grateful. It's not just reciprocal to another person, it's also to one's self. There is always something you can be grateful for. And, as Scott and Marla share, "When we open our eyes, first thing in the morning, we are so blessed. We have a roof, we have our bed, we have food and water, and we need to be grateful every second of the day. When we reflect on a circumstance in consideration of someone, who doesn't have a roof, is sleeping on the street, this perspective of what we have, the essential means for our well-being and not about what else we need, is the gratitude."

There's a gravity on the Intention Stick, and I always wear it, so people can see it. People will ask, "What is that?" I share with them what it is, right out of the gate; and they simply smile, and say, "That's awesome." This little spark of joy from sharing is the butterfly wing that can just cause this positive tsunami. You don't know where this person is coming from, or where they might be going. For them to see the necklace, and hear the good news and the positive story about the Intention Stick can change their whole pendulum in the other direction; in the upward, onward direction. This can really change their whole life – in this little spark – and I've seen this happen.

My Intention Stick also works in the reverse way. Sometimes I'm in a funk, and someone asks, "What is that?" The curiosity and question about my Intention Stick dissolves the funk – no matter the intensity of my inner dialogue, which caused the funk to begin with. "That's exactly what this is," I emphasize, "something that brings me back to a more positive reality." This moment, this reminder, gives me the opportunity to break away, to think, and reflect.

The Intention Stick is an amazing tool to wear, because it produces positive experience and connection; it either brightens someone else's day, or resets my day – away from the kind of funk I'm in. It's worn on my chest, over my heart, like a Superman vest. In a chaotic hurricane of life, such is the case in my job, or from my upbringing, this always adds a sense of positive calmness, a sense of joy, and a reflective place of positive light. Because this is very consistent and constant, it's why the Intention Stick is always on me. From a different light and point of view: it's like wearing a life jacket.

Soul Messenger
– 34 –

Jesse James Ferrell

Jesse is Founder of Jesse James Method
and Focus Four Me.

While attending a weekend workshop, as part of our adventure and journey for this event, a group of us visit Scott and Marla at their office. Something magical happens almost instantaneously upon walking in, and meeting them. I remember it vividly to this day; it's a feeling of being surrounded by a love that fills each and every person in the room. This feeling is so strong for me – I wept and wept.

I wait around for everyone else to leave; because I'm inspired to have a separate conversation with Scott and Marla. I express to them, I have always looked at life as everyone being connected as brothers and sisters. I'm immediately drawn to gifting Intention Sticks to all of my siblings, my mother, and my closest friends. I leave this day having purchased one for each of them, which I mail to them, as surprise gifts. As my family and friends receive them, it's lovely for me to hear their stories about which intentions they select.

Of all the intentions, I think my own favorites are *Love* and *Gratitude*, which I wear in combination with *Blessed* and *Health*. Love is the strongest energy we will ever experience and consume. It's only four letters, yet it's such a substantial word with such a great impact at the end of every day.

After receiving my Intention Stick, I have an experience with a friend who's having a seizure. I'm not sure what to do at this moment; so, I immediately ask Spirit to guide me. I place my hand on my friend's heart, and start blessing him with love. I'm saying over and over:

"I bless you with love, I bless you, and I love you."

Within fifteen seconds, his seizure completely stops. But once I take my hand off his heart, and stop blessing him, his seizures quickly come back. It's a powerful reminder of how simple it can be for us to impact others with this one Intention of *Love*.

In my work, treating chronic pain in the body, I begin every client session with a mental process of blessing them with love. Having an intention is where I start in my healing work, along with an understanding that we are made of energy. Even down to our cellular level, everything is energy.

Love is energy. I use the Intention of *Love* in my thoughts and prayers. And, when someone comes to mind, I immediately start blessing them with love. I know our thoughts are a powerful energy which can affect everyone around us. We can consciously choose our thoughts, as we consciously choose our intentions. The Intention Stick is able to guide our lives in a way which creates more peace and love.

I've observed the Intention Stick – to those I've gifted it to – become one more reminder of my connection with them. These are strong energetic connections, where I have the privilege of being able to ongoingly bless them with love; and gift them gratitude for their presence, and their impact on my life.

My sister, more frequently than anyone, switches out her intentions in her Intention Stick; because she likes to play with this dynamic energy. It has been fun and meaningful noticing what she experiences in her relationships with her family, her kids, and her grandkids. When she sets out to connect with them through conscious-awareness, this impacts how her life moves forward, in a positive way, by setting an intention for each of them.

The Intention Stick gifts someone, who may have lost hope, with the opportunity to have something tangible to hold onto. It becomes a reminder: "Somebody loves me enough at this moment." And this feeling that someone loves you can prevent them from taking their life, or prevent them from making a choice they will later regret. It's important to gift Intention Sticks to people, to continue spreading the message: that intention which we focus on does make a difference in our thoughts, our actions, and our lives.

THE INTENTION OF
FAITH ARRIVES ...
– 35 –

Kevin Wilkinson

*Kevin is owner of the New Dawn Group,
founder of the Living Full Project. Men's Coach,
Hypnotherapist and all-round good guy.*

M y catchphrase is "create life by design – not by default." In
my everyday life, I work in the investment field. I'm also
a hypnotherapist and a coach. Working with people is my passion
– the extent to which my clients feel as if they're my best friends.

My dear friend, Matt, gifts me an Intention Stick, and I lose it
while we're hiking in Arizona. The day before I return to the UK,
I contact Scott and Marla to purchase another Intention Stick.

"You didn't lose your Intention Stick. In fact, someone
else found your Intention Stick who needed it more than you
did ... And, without knowing it, you've gifted your Intention
Stick to someone else," Scott shares.

"I know there's a strong connection," Marla emphasizes.
"We're going to work together to do something meaningful."
This resonates with me; and is exactly what happens ...

* * *

For the last three years, I've been traveling with my clients to Bali on retreats. I gift my clients, who participate in these retreats, with an Intention Stick; because we are always creating our reality. So, why not be conscious of doing this?!

It's the last day of the retreat in Bali – and with a month in advance to ship the package of Intention Sticks to where we are – the Intention Sticks haven't arrived yet. In this village, where, for the first time, we are gifting these Intention Sticks to each of our clients, we ask for the Intention of *Trust* from the universe that the Intention Sticks will, in fact, arrive ...

An hour before our departure from the retreat, the package of Intention Sticks is delivered. Scott and Marla kindly give a talk, and articulate, through this video conference, the meaning behind each intention; so, my clients can learn how to select and share their intentions. The whole theme of our retreat has been based on *faith*, and surrender; which is to say, our patience for the Intention Sticks to arrive in Bali has become the essence of this experience.

In my own Intention Stick, I wear the Intentions of *Faith*, *Health*, and *Blessed*. Each morning, my Intention Stick sets a tone for the day. This is why the Intention Stick profoundly reso- nates with me. And, by wearing it so close to the heart, it's a powerful reminder.

* * *

Because I suffer from arthritis in my hips, the medical staff who assists me, shares that I will need a double hip replacement. I am forty-six years old, which means I will need to experience this procedure twice. And I sincerely don't want to proceed with the first surgery, in any case.

This circumstance has become an incredible amount of stress for me; and the alternatives to hip replacement (allegedly) will not work. So, I stop and pray, and hold my Intention Stick in my hands, close to my heart, and take some deep breaths – allowing the words of intention to resonate over me. Then, something appears in my news feed about a clinic in London, who's offering a new procedure involving stem cells ...

I travel to London, to confirm if this is an option that will, or will not, work for me. Based on this approach, I can move forward with this alternative procedure. However, it will cost nearly eight thousand pounds; from which I don't have the financial stability to therefore cover the overall costs.

This is where the Intention of *Faith* arrives ... I receive a phone call, which results in saving my client's investment. And, in turn, this means I receive a higher commission; thus, the money I need (with an additional fifty pounds over the total cost) to move forward with the procedure without surgery; and, therefore, I will gain mobility in my hips.

There's an element of surrender in this story: the time I spend to really connect with my Intention Stick, to feel its surge of energy, and to bring me back into alignment. The frequencies are here, and match my intentions. You have to feel good about what it is you're praying for – and resonate with the kind of intentions you select, share, and wear. This is a beautiful kind of alchemy ...

Some of the challenges and divisions which we face – whether it's race-relations, Coronavirus, internal, political, and/or religious conflicts – are all underpinned by fear. On the opposite side of this is unity, oneness, wholeness, and knowing that we are all the same. I feel unity is actually expanding more and more to the degree which consciousness continues to grow and expand.

There will come a time when there is a tipping point, if we continue to allow these constructs (the challenges and divisions) to divide us. So, as we deepen our practices, and strengthen our prayers, unity is what's going to keep us together.

Most people change something in their life when they've had enough, if they're sick and tired of receiving the same results. This seems to be happening on a collective level.

The first step for change is to align with our true selves, and maintain our actions from there. So, if we can shift our perspective, in the sense, as Dr. Wayne Dyer suggests: "when we change the way we look at things, the things we look at change."

Despite the nonsense which we're subjected to, it's exceptionally necessary to have the Intention of *Faith* that consciousness is increasing, growing, and expanding. And it's necessary to have the Intention of *Health* for ourselves, for the planet, and for our loved ones. It is also necessary to have the Intention of *Blessed*, ... that we are here, at this time, to witness and experience this increase in consciousness; and to be an active part of this change.

No matter the distance in between – the amount of miles we're away from one another – we can create something so beautiful; such that it's a testament to how powerful we are as a *collective*, rather than as individuals. We cannot escape this rising consciousness: if we remain true to who we are, if we become our own sovereign leader, and if we let this resonate outward; because we're here, right now, to specifically do this. What a beautiful time to be alive.

(In Loving Memory of Kevin Leroy Wilkenson)

Note to Reader from Scott and Marla

* * *

Nine months prior to our dear friend, Kevin, (who passed away on June 15th, 2021), this conversation instilled the Intention of *Faith* within us to open up our eyes to the love of brotherhood.

We can overlook the heart and soul, and look to the external. And all the conditioning of religion, politics, gender inequality, and the divisions which have been created from these challenges, as Kevin emphasizes, and shares with us, has softened through the kindness of his heart; as it gives us clarity to see, and look to the internal – the heart and soul within each of us, and thus look inside within ourselves, and by extension the people who surround us, from this point of view.

Through our heart and soul, we can connect with others in a more substantial way; something that has meaning, and love, which will endure.

THE TREE OF IMMORTALITY
– 36 –

Fernando Vossa

Fernando is an ascension artist building a lightship
to transform the body and the mind into a leading
edge human for planetary liberation.

We are living in the age of awakening. It's beautiful to be here, as a part of this exponential tribe, known as the Tree of Life Movement. Because we are all being called to create our best projects: the vision that's been an ever-inspiring light in our lives – for us to achieve. This is that moment.

When Scott and Marla share the Intention Stick, which has the Tree of Life sculpted on it, they demonstrate what's possible through the beauty of the design. This dialogue about the Tree of Life – and what it is – shows up many years ago in my art work: "Eating from The Tree of Immortality." As we talk about scripture, in various religious traditions, there is always a description of the Tree of Life.

The Tree of Life, for me, is connecting with the message of Creator, being an infinite being of light: the true self-realization; so we can "know thy self." We are this unimaginable source – we are a voice of light. So, to encapsulate this into a technology, I see this as a conscious intention to telepathically unite with others. We have energetically connected with our own intentions, so each one of us has a voice within the Tree of Life. This is to say, we're an expression of the Tree of Life – and we have chosen to unite as a tribe of light.

Marla and Scott have established a platform – to select a thought, and turn it into something you can touch and hold – which is accelerated materialization; and, by doing so, they have created it into something you can select, share, and wear. There's a distinction between manifesting and materializing something which you can select, share, and wear in the physical reality. The Tree of Life Movement is about transferring and transmuting our thoughts and desires, so we can heal the trauma of our life; from which we can release the stories we've been told – about why we're here – to, therefore, look at *the real truth of our most honest reality.*

As a scientist of Consciousness, as an explorer of dimensions, if you consider the vocabulary, (the twenty-two intentions which can be placed inside the Tree of Life Intention Stick), – to consider how many combinations of twenty-two intentions you can attend to and shape – a combinational explosion occurs. This twenty-two intention vocabulary, to me, represents codes and modules which are packages of light, and are multi-dimensional. In my current three-word combination – as a more holistic intention, representing the physical, mental, emotional, and spiritual connection – are the Intentions of *Light (the Light of Creativity)*, *Inspire*, and *Oneness.*

Each combination of intentions you create and develop is a body of knowledge; this activates your thoughts, and opens up areas of the heart as vocabulary that has a symbol, which is energetic; such as in the sense of hearing a sound. As each person picks their trinity, (their first three-intention combination), they become deeply connected with the combination they select.

What can we embody from these twenty-two intentions, so they become multi-generational? As mantras, families can hand them down to their children, just like families can hand down a mantle of skills, or a family business.

How about gifting your children an energetic footprint on Earth to continue the process of awakening, and healing; and all of the other possibilities of humans that are not taught in schools! Imagine if our children are in an environment where, in response to all the beautiful, insightful, and controversial things they say, the first response from their parent's or teacher's is, "I like that, tell me more," so they feel encouraged to share. This is a test, anytime a friend or person presents a new idea to you – a new concept they wish to explore – about something they want to do, what is your first response? The first thing ought to be: why do you find merit in this idea? If you don't have the capacity to arrive with one genuine reason why you like this controversial idea, you don't have the right to criticize or dispel it. This is to say, you don't have the right to cast it away; because you obviously don't understand the idea in your heart.

In the 1960s and 70s, a teacher might encounter one super star child in their entire career – if they're fortunate. The situation, now, is that teachers have super star children in all of their classrooms, and each of them are full of ideas to help change the planet for the better. The ascended masters are back in their little bodies of awakening: so, if you have a conversation with a three-year-old, a five-year-old, or a ten-year-old, they will straighten your clock out fast.

We've tuned in to the voice of Creator with the Tree of Life Intention Stick; and the voice of the planet is speaking to us. It's gifting us all the knowledge and information we request. When I know other people are wearing their Intention Stick, they have a level of awareness, of inquiry, of seeking connection, of sharing their vision and their projects. This creates a field of love, and a field of resonance. And, this starts revealing to us: how does this life work?

The other side of this veil is an expression of unity-consciousness. So, when you do reach this level to ask more meaningful questions – what happens? What will our life be like, when our entire tribe is united? What will it be like, when we declare ourselves healed? We are fully awakened-infinite beings of light.

When you look up at the night sky, you're looking at infinity: an unexplainable phenomenon. You're looking at something that has no ending. If you would like to know what your soul looks like, go outside at night and look up at those trillions of galaxies, and visualize them – as if your vision is perfect. This refers to cosmic heart vision, and you will see it all: look at the Universe as it is; this is who we are. The energy which created the Universe is inside each one of us. It is in our cells. So, feel the freedom to ask the biggest questions. And, when you ask, invoke your cosmic voice: invoke your piece of Creator; the part of God which each of us are.

The second stage of asking deep questions is to practice your creative ability. This occurs with something very powerful: an advanced skill. It's called "suspended judgment." Ask a question, create an empty space of silence, and see what's the first thing that comes to mind. Your body and your energetic version of you speaks in images and in emotions. Yet, how do you know? Because your cells have chills and goosebumps. This is when your whole body-planet is talking together; and this is the voice we've ignored our whole lives.

When you go through an awakening process at any level, you go through the first part: where you realize, a lot of what you've been taught, are lies. The second part: where you're inspired to discover that which is possible in your own life – what's possible from the heart. The third part, after this activation, is the intention, the focusing of the lens, of creating an aperture, where everything has to go through; this is the intention-stage of an awakened – or awakening – human.

The intention stage of awakening is the step right before you become a lucid being of love, which defines everything you do. The Intention Stick is the way to amplify the heart center; creating a field for our lens, on the way we see the world; it is a GPS for the map, which has been laid out for us, from the whole, from Creator. And, through our intentions, the only thing within which can guide us is our own intuitive connection to ourselves. Listen to the voice of Creator; who is resonating inside of you. Imagine what it will be like, when we are fully awakening infinite beings of light; and, at this very moment, we are inside the Intention Stick of Creator!

INTENTION BRINGS ATTENTION
– 37 –
Warren and Chloe Archer

*Warren is a captain for a major airline. a speaker,
an author, a pianist, and the founder of the
'I Think, Therefore I Lie' technique. Chloe is a
creative soul, a writer, a mixed-media artist,
a wife, and the mother of four boys.*

Warren:

The most beautiful things in life arise when we dissolve our expectations. In Transcendental Meditation, Maharishi suggests, "What you put your attention on – grows." So, within the Tree of Life Movement, the tree needs to be watered with intention, from which your attention arrives. As you wear the Tree of Life Intention Stick, this is a means to help free yourself through the intentions you place inside. All three of us, including our eight-year-old son, Teddy, wear Intention Sticks.

In my experience, the steps people choose to end their suffering are sometimes games they're playing with themselves, merely motions they're going through; without the real, genuine intention to end your suffering, or to be open to unconditional love, the mere attempt to try something is not nearly the same as the faith of doing something. So, if your intention is there, it will work – because your intention brings attention, and is what gifts the Intention Stick its magic.

If we consider the Intention of *Faith*: you simply have true faith in whatever is happening, is for you, and not merely happening to you. In *I Think, Therefore I Lie* (ITTIL) Technique, the distinction between belief and faith is "Faith transcends thought and is not based on reasoning. If reasoning is used to support faith, then by definition, it isn't faith, it's a belief."

The ITTIL Technique works simply by eliminating all belief in a thought. It's not the case, we say, "I'm going to take a leap of belief." Rather, we emphasize, "a leap of faith." Thus, we have the freedom to live in faith. And, therefore, the faith of trusting the moment.

Chloe:

If you have faith the Intention Stick is going to work, then it's going to work. If a person wears it, and thinks it's not going to work, then it's not going to work. There is no room for doubt in faith. That's why I've been wearing the Intention of *Faith* for a long time. Because I really want certain things in my life to happen. If you have faith, they certainly will.

I think it's very important that we have faith in ourselves. If you are not true to yourself, and have no love of self, and don't have faith in yourself, then you can't have faith in others; you can't help, or be someone who can positively influence others in any meaningful way.

The first thing we should do as people is to provide ourselves with some room to breathe; to not do things that society emphasizes we should – or shouldn't – do. We have to love ourselves when we're making mistakes, when we're not perfect, and when we're down; and, therefore, not only love ourselves when we're succeeding. This is unconditional love. It's only our thinking, which leads us to think we are imperfect.

Warren:

In *The Biology of Belief*, Bruce Lipton explains how cells receive their input from the periphery; and how everything around it thus reprograms the proteins. Lipton demonstrates, in a very fascinating way, how everything is interconnected: we are aligned in this way, and consist of trillions of cells; to the extent in which all of these cells interact with each other, and with their environment. Furthermore, we're not separate from the environment around us: from the air we breathe, the food, and water; all these things, thus have an effect.

As Chloe likes to point out and suggest: our bodies are little universes. The cells work together like the planets. We are part of the universe. We work together and have armies of cells that work together; when one of them goes wrong is when the person becomes sick.

If you are constantly putting your attention on negative thoughts, if you're a pessimist because you count on things going wrong, not realizing you're creating a self-fulfilling prophecy, you're actually changing your physiology at a cellular level by doing this. Society teaches us to trust negative thoughts. We're not taught to think in terms of faith and love, or any of the words that can be found in the Intention Stick.

As a result, the words in our Intention Stick can have an even more powerful effect on us when we use them, and bring them into action. Why is it more powerful? Because we are conditioned to this negativity; and when we switch, the contrast is so great that we see it as a miracle. It's not a miracle, really. It's just a normal way of living. On a superficial level, things might seem different; but on the level where things really matter, they're not. This interconnectedness is part of the beauty of the Tree of Life Movement.

A METAPHOR TO
STAY PRESENT
– 38 –

Bart Scholeissen

*Bart is a former neuroscientist and
neuropsychologist, founder at Back to Your
Nature coaching, Wim Hof Method Academy
Instructor, father, guide, and nature lover.*

While living in Poland, as one of the academy instructors
in the Wim Hof Method, Mark Johnston (who introduces
me to the Intention Stick) and I strengthen our bond as we travel
upward, through the mountains, and practice cold exposure,
breathwork, and mindset training. Which, as a substantial part
of the process in learning the Wim Hof Method, is where, for the
first time, I recognize the necklace Mark's wearing.

Nearly two weeks later, a package arrives at my front door.
From the other side of the world, Mark sent, both Wim and I, as
a gift, an Intention Stick. As I wear my Intention Stick, I like to
select my intentions from a feeling of what I'm connecting with;
sometimes I will shift the intentions around, and other times,
they will stay the same. This depends on what arises in my life.

When people ask what's around my neck, I share the story of how this is a meaningful tool, and how the Tree of Life symbol is a connection with self, with one another, and with nature. I believe that we are all one; we are made of the same stardust as nature around us; and I think the energy which we radiate, may go further than one mile from where we are…

We are part of this global tribe, the Tree of Life Movement – and the connections are global; yet, they might even be interstellar. I would never have connected with Scott and Marla on the other side of the globe, if I never changed something inside, and let go of my own limiting beliefs.

Life can sometimes feel dogmatic. Do this, or don't do this. Or I'm supposed to be happy, or I'm supposed to look good on the outside. All these dogmas – from which I used to think, "I'm not good enough" or "I don't belong…" – cloud my mind, and clarity. It's important for me to realize that this sense of darkness, or any sense in which darkness can pertain to life, is a part of life; just as light is.

I compare this relation of darkness and light to the mountaintops and valleys within nature; that valleys only exist because of the mountaintops. So, we need this fluctuation – of light and darkness. We need to go up and down, and strive for positivity and gratitude each day. This doesn't mean we need to – or have to – be happy each day. For me, working with intention, and learning from it, means being open to the moments when I'm not my most happy, energized self. I believe it's the journey, with all of its ups and downs, which makes life interesting.

The Intention Stick helps encourage someone on their journey, and their connection with life – because it's a physical reminder – because it's tangible. You can touch it, you can feel it, there are intentions inside. You can use it as a metaphor, as a tool, as an anchor to be present in the moment. There are lots of ways to connect life with the Intention Stick.

I'm grateful to have the awareness, and the anchors to help me come back, to arrive, and exist in this present moment; this is how the Intention Stick helps me connect and interact within my life and its lessons. And I believe everything is a lesson; that this whole life we are living – this incredible experience – is one big learning lesson.

ARRIVE FROM LOVE
– 39 –

Jeffrey C. Olsen

Jeffrey is a best-selling author, international speaker,
a near-death experiencer, spiritual leader,
survivor, husband, father and friend.

I n my heart is *Oneness* – to realize we have far more in common, than we do separately, as human beings. Our experiences
are so diverse, and this diversity creates beauty. It's our uniqueness which brings such perfection. We have to embrace our
uniqueness and our differences, so we can really come together
in this sense of *Oneness*: this is a significant intention of mine.
And then, there is the Intention of *Gratitude*.

My journey to these realizations began more than twenty
years ago, when my family and I had a horrific automobile accident. It was in the Spring, around Easter time: I was driving.
My wife Tamara had reclined her seat back, and was sleeping;
our two sons, seven-year-old Spencer, and our toddler, fourteen-
month-old Griffin, were in the backseat; and Griffin was strapped
into his car seat.

My biggest fear, the hardest part of the story, is I believe I
just dozed off at the wheel ... we were going seventy-five miles

an hour on cruise control. I swerved to the right, and overcorrected to the left, lost control, and the car rolled over; six, seven, eight times.

Because Tamara's seat was reclined, the seat belt didn't properly restrain her, and she suffered a severe head trauma, which took her life. The car seat broke apart, and Griffin was ejected from the car, taking his life. I blacked out during the high-speed rollover, and when I regained consciousness, I could hear Spencer crying hysterically in the backseat. I struggled to attend to him, and realized I was pinned in the wreckage. I was in severe pain and couldn't breathe. Somehow, I knew that both Tamara and Griffin were gone. It's almost like Spirit had said to me that they were gone. I don't even know how to articulate that. I also realized that Spencer was going to be fine.

I'm losing consciousness, half my family is gone, I was driving the car, and I was consumed with an overwhelming feeling of guilt ... can't I just take back those two seconds? This was the worst experience – the worst kind of hell – a person should ever be in; and, it was in that moment, suddenly, everything became calm. I felt like light came to a very dark situation. It felt as if this light came to me, like a comforting blanket, and I felt myself rising up above the scene of the accident. Suddenly, I could breathe again, and the pain was gone. I felt quite surprised.

There I was, in this intense light, feeling fantastic, except I was aware of what had gone on. Suddenly, in the light, Tamara, my wife who was deceased next to me, was also in the light with me. She was standing with me and speaking to me. She looked absolutely gorgeous, and radiant. She said to me, emphatically, "Jeff, you've got to go back. It's not your time." If I didn't go back, our seven-year-old would've been orphaned. I made the choice to come back. I said the most profound goodbye I will ever say. With the intention to come back, I found myself wandering around a hospital, in this bubble of light. I had no concept of time. I just knew I had wrecked the car, half of my family was gone, and I had told my wife goodbye.

As I found myself wandering around a hospital, I was seeing doctors, nurses, patients, and the families of patients. I believe this is what changed me forever; because it didn't matter who they were, or what they had done, I saw them as these glorious siblings. It's like I knew them. I knew them perfectly. I knew their lives, their loves, their hates, their challenges, and what had happened to them. There was this absolute feeling of oneness; experiencing oneness beyond anything I had ever comprehended. There was a feeling of connection to everyone around me in such a profound way: I became them, and they were me. There was absolute perfect empathy and unconditional love.

Finally, I came up to a body laying on a gurney. I looked down at it, only to realize – that's me … except it was not me. I was still having this profound connected experience of oneness. That was my body, my skin suit of flesh; and, yet, I realized I am not my body. As this was happening, I had a profound realization of what a gift our body is to us – what a miracle our bodies are. My body was now a wreck, and would never be the same again.

Again, I made the choice to return to my body; and with the intention of getting back in that body, I plunged back into that dense, heavy grief, pain, torment, guilt, all of it. Rescuers had been able to extract Spencer from the wreckage. He was banged up and didn't have any life-threatening injuries. They airlifted me to the closest trauma center hospital. Both of my legs were crushed, and my left leg had to be amputated above the knee. My back was broken, my right arm was torn off, my lungs collapsed, and the seatbelt had cut through my lower abdomen, rupturing my intestines. I was in critical condition. They kept me in the hospital for more than four months, where I underwent eighteen surgeries.

When I was brought home from the hospital, I was so worried about my son, Spencer. He had lost his mother, his brother, and in many ways, he lost his father, too. I was never going to be the same. I was in a wheelchair, and had been fitted with a prosthetic limb; how is he going to deal with this?

When it was finally time to return home, my two big brothers, who were so loving of me, picked me up out of the car and placed me in the wheelchair. I could see Spencer looking out the window of our house, watching. As they pushed me in the wheelchair, up the driveway, Spencer came running out of the house, running towards me; and then, ran right past me. I thought to myself, "it must have been too much for him to see his dad this way;" one leg chopped off, the other one in a brace, and his arm in a sling.

When I turn my wheelchair around to see where he went, my seven-year-old son, who's across the street, was knocking on our neighbor's door saying, "come out, come out, my dad made it home, come see my dad!" Spencer turns back, and runs to me, throws himself on my lap, and wraps his arms around me. "I'm going to be like this, but I am going to work very hard to get well."

* * *

Eventually, I fell in love again, and remarried. My wife Tanya is the hero of my story. She shared love with me, unconditionally. Spencer grew up to be an incredible young man. He married a woman who just loves the Intention Stick. When I received my Intention Stick, I chose the Intention of *Oneness*.

Love is the most powerful force in the Universe. We arrive from love, and it will conquer everything. It can overcome hate, and separateness. And we may not necessarily always see the connection; but we are one: we are brothers and sisters. The

Divinity is in every one of us. If we stand arm and arm, this whole world will change; and transform in such a way where Heaven will be here. So, when I speak about gratitude, unconditional love, and oneness, this isn't a philosophy which I read in a book … I experienced it in such a profound way that it has forever changed my life, and my perspective.

Always Up For
An Adventure!
– 40 –

Tina Bennett

*Tina is Founder of Vanilla Swirl, Executive Pastry
Chef, Mother of Three, Spiritual Healer for
animals and humans, Resident Activities
Director to Blind/Autistic adult son.*

True to who my son is, he's always up for an adventure! My son Hollywood and I have the pleasure of visiting Scott. Hollywood has no idea why we are going to meet Scott at his office. So far, the best part about arriving at this office building is a ramp near the entrance; and we have to entertain this playful moment before we can enter the building: Hollywood spends nearly ten minutes running back and forth, up and down the ramp until he's out of breath.

This adventure gets better and better when we walk into the elevator, and travel up ten floors. I describe the story this way, because Hollywood truly loves the simple things most people don't seem to notice. To see the world through Hollywood brings me peace and joy. You can't help but smile as you watch him.

Hollywood is a very spiritual person. He believes in manifestation; and Hollywood will often go into his room to nap, so he can travel. He describes it as closing his eyes, and traveling in a world where he can see. Hollywood has Autism, and cannot see in the physical world; yet, the world in which he can see, is a peaceful place with lots of "ploppage" as Hollywood likes to call it ("ploppage," which we refer to as rain). He actually writes down his dreams when he awakens, and we discuss them almost daily. Hollywood doesn't want to see in this physical world, and he is adamant about it. "I'm here to see things differently," Hollywood says, "and I chose you to be my mom to help me."

We have long conversations about this, and about why his identical twin brother, Jonathan (who died when he was three months old), is with him. Hollywood has never had friends come over, and doesn't connect with people in this way, which is part of his Autism. He always has Jonathan with him, Hollywood says; and so, he's never alone.

Yet, even with being a person who likes to be alone, Hollywood's dream is to own a motorhome that we drive around with our four pets, and meet people everywhere we travel; all the while checking out the weather patterns as we go. Hollywood just wants to shake people's hands, so he can feel their heart, and, even more, so they can feel his heart.

As a child, Hollywood was bullied in elementary school, suspended in 2nd grade, 5th grade; and, in high school, for 'inappropriately' holding a girl's hand. More than anything, he wants to meet people. He can tell right away if the person is "good" or "safe." And, if he's uncomfortable in any way, he will pull back and his body will become stiff.

When we walk into Scott's office, Hollywood immediately stands tall and has a smile on his face. You can feel it – even if his face was covered with a mask! He immediately connects with

Scott, and sits down to get to know him. Again, Hollywood has no idea why we're here.

On my son's right is my dear friend, Bari, who introduced me to Scott; and Scott's wife, Marla, is on Zoom, so she can participate as well. Also, Emma, who is an amazingly talented young lady, who I think the world of, is on Zoom, calling in from the University of Arizona. The room is full of love.

Scott describes the Tree of Life Movement, and shares with us how it all began. Hollywood, who typically fidgets when sitting in one place for any period of time, doesn't fidget – and doesn't move. When Scott says something which resonates with him, he reaches over to me and squeezes my arm. It's so much fun to watch, because my son doesn't connect with a lot. So, this is a big day! I have tears in my eyes the entire time I sit there watching him.

After Scott and Marla share their story of what they're doing with the Tree of Life Movement, Scott asks my son if he has any questions. "How can I help?!" is Hollywood's response. I've never heard Hollywood listen to something, to someone who's sharing something, and want to help because of it. Scott presents Hollywood with his own Intention Stick for his thirty-second birthday, and he selects the intentions to place inside after Scott reads all twenty-two intentions to choose from; as Hollywood is listening to the intentions, he reaches over and squeezes my arm when a word resonates with him. Hollywood chooses the Intentions of *Love*, *Joy*, *Happiness*, and *Faith*.

The best part is … I knew the words he selected. Not only does this validate how sweet Hollywood's Soul is, but his intentions are truly to have *faith*, be *happy*, and spread *love* and *joy*. Scott and Marla select Hollywood's last intention to place inside his Intention Stick; which is the Intention of *Inspire*. My son loves this word. It's such an amazing experience!

Since this experience, Hollywood comes up to me several times a day, and describes what he wants to do with these words of intention, and how much stronger he feels with them. I've had my own amazing experiences with my Intention Stick since my friend Bari gifted one to me last year.

Everyone has their own beliefs and ways to motivate themselves, either personally or professionally. I have always been a spiritual person, and I write down my goals and place pictures up for motivation. I believe the Intention Stick has a power of its own, and I am so grateful to Scott and Marla for what they're doing. There's something so incredibly powerful with having your intentions laying over your heart. I believe people come into our lives for a reason, and I am blessed and grateful for the ones who have come into mine; who have made my life so much better.

THE DIVINE ENERGY WITHIN
– 41 –

Melissa Macias, M.D., Ph.D.

*Melissa is a Ph.D. neurobiologist and
neurosurgeon, NASA researcher, and serves
on the Tree of Life board of directors.*

I'm guided to this beautiful rock with a perfectly symmetrical round hole. This is the moment I realize, like the rock, I have a hole in my heart; and it's been there ever since my mom died: my world had been shattered when she died.

My whole family structure changed when I was twenty years old; and instead of being able to fill this hole with intellectualization, philosophy, and nature, as I like to do, it created a wider, more substantial hole and inner void.

I arrive at this realization that there is a hole in all of our hearts. This hole has been placed in our hearts by Creator; and, only, Creator can fill the hole. We are all on a journey together, so we can learn and share and understand this philosophy with one another. It's similar to the understanding that as we walk through a labyrinth, every step is intentional – in a direction to the center and core of who we are. And, as we walk in this direction, we have to surrender to these steps as we move forward.

I'm at a place in my life where I'm discovering that we create the intention – the will of our decision – and the free will to affirm: "I will stay on this path; and I trust every step on this path will guide me." Because there's always been this void and a hole in my heart, nothing really resonates with me, and my entire journey, after the passing of my mom, has been spent looking and searching.

After overcoming my initial resistance to Dr. Lynn Crocker's meditation, chanting, and yoga, I recognize this as the direction and path I need to be on … it resonates with me, and provides me with a spark, which I've never felt before … I've found something that's filling my heart.

"I would like to gift you something," Lynn says. Lynn unclasps her Intention Stick, and I feel this cosmic jolt of energy the moment I receive it. I know it's charged with an amazing frequency, because of Lynn's incredible spiritual practices. Lynn shares with me the twenty-two words, the seventy-two meanings of each intention, and the frequencies (the resonance of these words of intention), so I can select three intentions to place inside my Intention Stick.

The first intention I choose is *Faith*, because most of my journey has been searching for something beyond my work as a physician, which I can believe in; to help guide me, and to help heal me. My second intention is *Health*, because without health, we really can't achieve anything. If we have our health, we can always have the free will and energy to stay in alignment, and thus stay on our path. My third intention is *Success*, though not success in a material way; and, because of the hole I used to feel, I've achieved this success in filling the void in my heart.

Through my discussions with Lynn, we talk about what meditation really is, what the Intention Stick is, (which is a meditation of intentions you keep close to your heart); how you constantly interact with your electromagnetic field, even when you're not thinking about it; and how this manifests in you, and resonates with you. We talk about the frequency of words, the frequency of good words and the frequency of bad words, and how these frequencies interact with our energy levels. This is all very powerful, and meaningful.

By speaking words of intention – *Faith, Hope, Success, Love* – this brings your body vibration to a different alignment, even if it's for a minute, or even if it's forever. I believe every individual has a divine self, and can choose to tap into this divine self we've been gifted from Creator. This is a divine energy within; and with the energetic intent you set, you don't have to be conscious of this every day; because the words in the Intention Stick help you in the energetic realm at all times.

As a scientist, this, as many scientists and great minds have understood throughout the ages, is about energy. All we're talking about is our bio-energy, and how we connect to our energetic Earth and our energetic cosmos. I think there is a direct connection. It's the energy you surround yourself with, it's the energy you consume, and it's the energy you resonate with, which makes a difference in the energetic fields you expose yourself to; and this is going to drive the biochemical processes in the body.

Because I think that we should be able to measure what is shifting and changing, I plunged myself back into my Ph.D. world to do an amazing literature search; combing through the different studies. Through this study research, and meeting Scott and Marla, we organized a protocol so we can actually look at the changes; from brain waves to biofeedback, as a person is in a practice or an experience, in order to observe and document these energy shifts. There is a lot of fascinating, and wonderful research work that is happening in recognizing this reality, and we're thrilled and honored to be a part of it.

"What is that necklace you're wearing?" my patients often ask me. When I share the story of the Intention Stick with them, they're in awe. I've gifted Intention Sticks to my patients, and you can see their face change, and the energy of the person morph.

One particular patient will always stand out in my heart.

When he was incarcerated, he had a seizure in prison. He was brought to our hospital where he was found to have a large brain tumor, and would need surgery. He had been stabilized with medications when I spoke with him.

"What is that around your neck?" he asks during our conversation. I share with him the story of the Intention Stick, and how you place your intentions inside. He stares at me with these beautiful, very kind eyes. I don't know what he's incarcerated for, nor do I care, because he is my patient. He really enjoys, and appreciates hearing the story behind the Intention Stick and the Tree of Life Movement. "I'd really like to have something like that, but I can't wear any jewelry in jail," he shares. Yet, he seems uplifted by our conversation.

Later this evening, I receive a phone call. He suddenly passed away from a blood clot in his lungs. I'm shocked, and dismayed by this news. The next morning, I arrive at the hospital, and speak with the nurses who were on duty when he passed away.

As we speak about him, suddenly, a beam of light swiftly radiates to the top of this wall above the doorway next to us. This greenish-purplish colored light dances along the wall, and then zooms outward. I'm stunned. "Did you all see that?" I exclaim. Everyone sees this flash of light dancing on the wall, and is shaken up by this; because there are no windows in the room, or any way for reflections to come in. And I feel, in this moment, an energy – a sense of peace.

I share what happened with Lynn, who has had many similar experiences with her own patients. She believes that I met this man, who was serving life in prison, for a reason. She senses that he had come to learn about his intention in life and reflect on it, so he could be set free. His soul needed to hear the story of the Intention Stick.

* * *

From my perspective, we're all on the brink of an elevation, and the Intention Stick can be a key component of our soul's journey. We're all here to serve: this is our purpose for being here. We just sometimes forget. And now, we're remembering!

CHILDREN ARE THE SEEDS
OF OUR FUTURE
– 42 –

"You may say I'm a dreamer, but I'm not
the only one ... I hope someday you'll join
us, and the world will live as one."
[John Lennon]

Marla:

It's March 22, 1996, and our second son, Justin, is born. Eight days later, Scott and I arrive at Phoenix Children's Hospital with Justin – in great haste!

Because the medical staff can't seem to pinpoint Justin's ailments – causing stomach sickness, which is also causing a severe level of jaundice – Justin's symptoms continue to become more intensified as every moment moves forward...

A medical team from California arrives at the hospital, yet for an entirely different reason. It appears to us, the real reason – the purpose of us being at this hospital – is for this medical team; so they can identify the overall cause. From which they attend to Justin, perform emergency surgery; and, thus, save Justin's life.

* * *

Children are the seeds of our future; because from them, are the seeds of their future: their children, our grandchildren, and great-grandchildren. The spiritual message which remains with us from day to day is for all of us to be arm-in-arm; to plant and water the seeds of positive intention; so, as to encourage and help our children (the children of our generation) grow in every way possible … thus, as to live a life of intention.

It is our obligation, it is our responsibility, to help strengthen the hearts and minds of our children. So, they learn and understand how to self-love, self-nurture, and self-care; how to look within and connect with self; how to overcome their circumstances in moments of sorrow and distress; and how to build, grow, and strengthen their life from their own intentions.

Even after children are provided with the essentials of food, water, and shelter, it is exceptionally important and necessary to continue onward and forward with them in a heartfelt way; to demonstrate how to create meaningful connection, so they connect (or reconnect) with their dreams and aspirations; as to not suppress their dreams and aspirations, based on one negative experience or multiple negative experiences, and their painful memories of these experiences.

Children often seem to disconnect and disassociate, based on negative experiences. Thus, they can't seem to find a connection to their dreams and aspirations, or can't seem to find a way back to reconnect and reassociate with their dreams and aspirations. Therefore, this sense of disconnection from their consciousness, from their inner self-awareness to be present, be inspired, and aspire to live with meaningful connection and positive intention with their self, family, and friends, discourages them to connect with a positive state of awareness and sense of self.

This disconnection from their sense of self, becomes the disconnect from their dreams and aspirations, and the inspiration to be authentic; to become a more authentic embodiment of who they are inspired and aspire to be; as an individual within the collective of humanity ...

If we merely walk away from our children, and do not continue to attend to them in a meaningful way, they will not have the appropriate tools; to feel inspired and impelled to aspire in life. We believe it is our obligation, our responsibility, to ensure and make certain our children grow up living a life of positive intention; whether they are an orphan living in an orphanage; whether they are homeless, sleeping at a homeless shelter or on the street; or whether they come from a family of privilege and wealth; because every child is at-risk and faces their own unique challenges, i.e. the kinds of obstacles and concerns they experience, as it relates to their own life story.

Through this point of view, from the perspective to develop, encourage, and support our children in a meaningful way, we can guide, help, and lead them to a place where they acknowledge and understand they are loved, they matter, have purpose, and are as important as everyone else in this world.

When a child ages out of an orphanage, or when a parent, mentor, or therapist is not by their side to be a guiding hand, then the appropriate tools and thoughtful reminders to self-love and have courage, as they wear their Intention Stick, are there to strengthen, improve, and focus upon.

The connection they create with the person who gifts them the guidance of intention, gifts them a heartfelt, soul-to-soul connection. As a child continues onward, they will remember this connection, this heartfelt message which will help, encourage, and inspire them to help, inspire, and encourage children who are less fortunate; so, they too will stay on the path of positive intention (from any positive intention which resonates with them ...) to *Inspire*, to *Love*, to have *Courage*, and to be *Happy*.

* * *

We recall the story of John Lennon, before his fame; before the Beatles, when John is five years old. John states, in an interview: "When I was five years old, my mother always told me that happiness was the key to life. When I went to school, they asked me what I wanted to be when I grew up. I wrote down 'happy'. They told me I didn't understand the assignment, and I told them they didn't understand life."

John is just a child. And this, rather than choosing to be a doctor, a lawyer, or a fireman, he simply writes on his piece of paper, that he aspires to be *happy*.

Yet, here is a teacher telling him that he doesn't understand the assignment ... (as if our assignment in life is to be anything other than happy ...).

It's significant, and important to teach our children, so they learn to be exceptionally wary of the people whom they share their aspirations and inspiring thoughts with; because children can become discouraged by the people who are, as it were, dream killers.

It happens from time to time, when people share their opinions in a rather discouraging way, whether one asks them or not. Thus, we ought to be careful when listening to the negativity; because the negativity from others can become a distraction and become exceptionally discouraging (whether or not we give them the power, or merely don't have the inner strength to overcome the negativity, i.e. the negative thoughts and opinions of others).

So, surround yourself with people who inspire and uplift you to become the best version of who you are; because, if so, the sky's the limit! Our children are our future, and our children have a future ... and this world doesn't yet realize how brilliant these children are ... they are the seeds that will change the world. They are the light and the love that's going to eradicate all of the negativity and divisiveness which appears everywhere, around the world.

Through chaos and darkness, the light will shine through; and will connect every heart and soul, in every child in this world, together ... just as John Lennon emphasizes, and sings, "the world will live as one."

FROM A CHILD'S
POINT OF VIEW
– 43 –

Marla:

I t's 1996, our oldest son, Harrison, is two years old. Because of his sense of adventure, there is a small toy truck that Harrison would like to step into and drive. From our perspective, the outcome is obvious. Yet, from Harrison's point of view, he *believes* ... has *faith* ... is a soul who wants to explore ... and, is determined.

When we confine ourselves to a limited way of thinking, and have a direct influence on our children, this influence can diminish the endless possibilities with which our children can see; through the use of their own imagination; and therefore, to be creative and dream. Their minds are open to unique possibilities; and, at such a young age, children believe anything is possible. This child-like state of mind is limitless; we constantly witness this perspective in children who wear Intention Sticks ...

Scott:

One of our clients, who's inspired to gift Intention Sticks to their family and friends, has a four-year-old daughter, who inquires ...

"What about me, mommy?"

"No, sweetie, you're too young," the mother says.

So, I share a story, about our dear friends, Richard and Lisa, who gift Intention Sticks to their two eldest sons ... "what about us?" their two youngest son's Tanner and Jacob inquire.

"You have to earn them by writing a letter about what the Tree of Life Movement, and what the Tree of Life Intention Stick mean to you," Richard and Lisa add. Tanner, who's seven-years-old, sends us the following letter:

The story is about love. The Tree of Life means happiness. The Tree of Life means not to hate and do good and to love. It's about not being selfish and not expecting things in return. The Tree of Life movement is about sending positive energy to myself and to other people.

Jacob, who's nine-years-old, writes in his letter:

I think the story is about a tree that loves a boy and wants to make him happy and the story is also about giving love and not expecting something back. The Tree of Life is a symbol that we are all connected to, so we share the same energy. Each leaf from the Tree of Life, stands for each person on Earth. I think the Intention Stick is about you put a word in the stick that it will bring it to your mind and then out into the universe. My first words are health and faith for my friend's mom, who is really sick.

After sharing this story, and letters Tanner and Jacob sent to us ... "of course you can have an Intention Stick," the mother says to her daughter. Her first three intentions are *Love, Peace,* and *Kindness.* Each time a three or four-year-old child receives an Intention Stick, they know instinctively what these Intentions of *Love*, *Peace* and *Kindness* are.

* * *

Our dear friend, Dr. Gladys McGarey, shares a story about her great granddaughter, Maggie May, who's four years old; "the other day she's fussing around, and finally, her parents say to her…"

"Maggie May, what's the problem?"

"I'm worried!"

"What are you worried about?" her parents ask.

"I don't know who I am."

"Honey, you're our daughter."

"But I don't know what I'm becoming."

"You have mommy, daddy, grandma, and God to help you learn what you're becoming."

Maggie May takes a deep breath; "that's the kindest thing you could have said to me, goodnight."

FOR THE WORLD
– 44 –

Scott:

*H*i-*Tops for Haiti* supports *Chances for Children*, a nonprofit child advocacy center focused on providing support "to these children – one child, one family, one community at a time." Each year, Blake and Caleb go door-to-door in their neighborhood and their friends' neighborhoods, so they can collect and gift donated shoes to the at-risk children.

Blake, who is thirteen years old, conceived the idea for their charity *Hi-Tops for Haiti* "because of my brother Caleb, who's adopted from Haiti. I wanted to emphasize two of my favorite things. So, I also infused my love of sports; the high tops refer to basketball. And this is where the name *Hi-Tops for Haiti* comes from," Blake says.

Marla and I gift Intention Sticks to Caleb, who is nine years old, and to Blake, at Blake's bar mitzvah. "I chose the Intention of *Faith*, because I wish there was more faith in the world. And when I don't believe in something, I think of the word I placed inside my Intention Stick, which lifts me up, and makes me believe … my intentions are true, powerful words," Caleb says.

"I also chose *Spiritual* because I just felt it was very strong at that moment; it's about believing in something. And I chose

Happiness because there is a lot of happiness in the world; and I just wanted to put that in my Intention Stick," Caleb shares.

"*Laugh/Joy* is one of my intentions. And if I'm mad at somebody, or if I'm in a bad mood because something happened, I can always just think of my Intention Stick. And this can just cheer you up," Blake emphasizes; "I've seen pictures of children, and even a picture of my brother, when he was younger. Many of them wore torn up shoes or didn't have shoes. Even if you don't have a platform like *Chances for Children*, you can always give to people; or you can always start your own thing – and create your own platform. You can always make a difference no matter how small it is … because it's still a difference."

* * *

Scott:
Rebeca Patrese is a Musician Living a Life of Intention. She is the first young woman who's been gifted an Intention Stick in Brazil. At this time, Rebeca is sixteen years old. She has been experiencing severe depression, when one of her online friends in Arizona tells her that she's going to send her a gift for her birthday; but doesn't tell her what the gift is …

"When I open the package, I immediately start to cry, because I feel so much love. I place the Intention Stick on, and I've never taken it off. I choose three words: *Happiness*, *Believe*, and *Peace*," Rebeca shares; "I have been broken and barely surviving. And these three words mean a lot to me. This is all I want for my life: I really want peace in my soul, and to believe anything is possible."

"Almost every person I meet asks: what is that shining on you? And I say: it's an Intention Stick, where I place three words that are my life; it's a symbol that what matters is inside your soul."

"I can feel the energy of the Intention Stick, and the love behind it. I have started to believe in things and in myself. It's incredible that a girl like me, in a country where most people don't know how to speak English, is the first person to have one."

"I show my cousins, and the children who play at the park close to my house, this Intention Stick. They place their attention on it and want to know what it is. So, I show them the intentions inside, and why I chose them."

"When I take my Intention Stick off to show them, they take it, so they can wear it; then they hold it, close their eyes tightly, and wish for something. Then, I'll ask: Did you make your wish? And they say: yes; yes, I did. Afterwards, I place it back on, and I can see them with a huge smile, as they go back to playing."

"They really do make their wish. It's so pure, and so beautiful that the Intention Stick calls to them … if you look at a picture of me from a year ago until now, I'm always wearing my Intention Stick. I will wear this forever, and I'm grateful to have this. I feel so happy, and blessed to be a part of this; because this makes me feel alive … I can finally be happy, believe, and have peace."

From a musically meaningful message, Yusuf Islam's viewpoint:

"*Now* I've been *happy* lately, thinking about the good things to come … and I believe it could be, something good has begun. I've been smiling lately, dreaming about the world as one … and I *believe* it could be, someday it's going to come."

[Cat Stevens, *Peace Train*]

THE AGE OF CELEBRATION
– 45 –

Scott:

"If you've forgotten how to be playful, just go be playful … you'll soon remember," Swami suggests; "Joy! Joy! Joy!"

Our dear friend, Swami the Orange Cowboy, describes to us how the notion "I'm getting too old" can lead to a downward spiral … "I hear a lot of my friends in their 70's and 80's, say to me: 'I'm getting older, I'm having a senior moment.' Which is why remembering to be childlike is more profound than you might think."

Swami's philosophy is about exercising the Intention of *Joy*. Swami emphasizes if you exercise the muscle of *Joy*, continuously, for twenty-one days, it will become a habit. And, therefore, you can experience the presence of *Joy*. And this, will help uplift your spirit …

"We are spirit," as Pierre Teilhard de Chardin suggests. "We are not human beings, having a spiritual experience. We are spiritual beings, having a human experience." So whichever intention you select, have an intention of spirit," Swami encourages.

"When it was time for me to change the intentions in my Intention Stick," Swami contemplates, "what's more substantial than the Intention of *Joy*?"

"I select the Intention of *Courage*, because this is a sobering word. It's the courage to create joy. The courage to be more of a light in the world. The courage to listen to everybody's point of view, because points of views can cause controversy. The courage to be quiet when people misunderstand you," Swami suggests; "courage becomes an empowering fuel of joy."

"My sense of leadership is to be joyful," Swami adds, "so you will be inspired to be joyful. As your heart becomes more open and vulnerable, it's helpful to consider the beautiful expression: 'there is more room to connect with your angels.' My angels hint at the age of joy: the age of celebration."

A PRAYER FOR PEACE
– 46 –

Scott:

"A Prayer for Peace" shares the meaning and strength of family connection. In this story, Kinslee Larue, Sherry's great-niece, is a newborn twin sister to her older sister, Paislee Sue, and has been diagnosed with a very rare (ATRT) cancer, after the doctors found a two-inch tumor at the base of her brain. Kinslee is undergoing MRI's, surgeries, and chemotherapy. As a newborn, the doctor's insights are such that there is a very slight chance of Kinslee surviving; because this type of cancer is aggressive; and based on these treatments at such a young age, there are medical issues which can potentially arise later in life.

Because Sherry does not live in the same state as her family (Kinslee's mom Jessica, dad Josh, older brother Brent, eldest sister Bralynn, and her twin sister Paislee), it has been an exceptionally traumatic time for Sherry, who works alongside our daughter, Addison, at a cancer research center in Arizona. Addison notices that Sherry doesn't seem as bright and cheerful as her energy normally is.

Sherry explains the full scope of Kinslee's well-being with Addison; from which our daughter is impelled to connect Sherry with me; to see if the Intention Stick will "bring some type of hope into her life." Addison shares the significance of what is happening, and invites Sherry to my office. We gift two Intention Sticks, and have an intention-based ceremony for Kinslee and for Sherry.

Sherry is inspired from this meaningful experience and gifts ten Intention Sticks to send to her family; from which they can create a family-based intention, blessing, and prayer together. When Sherry's family receives their Intention Sticks, we connect via Zoom as they're in the hospital room, holding an Intention Stick over Kinslee, Jessica's cell phone rings; it's one of the doctors.

Jessica steps away for this urgent phone call, receives the news they've been waiting for, and shares that Kinslee's twin sister, Paislee, and her siblings, Brent and Bralynn, do not have the genetic disposition for ATRT; these test results arrive mere seconds after everyone chooses their intentions, (while on Zoom), and places their Intention Sticks over their hearts. This gift – this blessing – arrives when the family is together; (as they select their intentions and say prayers for Kinslee's health and well-being.)

"We have overcome so much since the beginning and look forward to our little one being a beacon of hope to those that will and are battling this cancer currently," Kinslee's Grandpa Doug emphasizes. As they are all together, the family dynamic strengthens their thoughts, emotions, and state of mind for both Kinslee, and each other. It's an incredible moment to see their family say a prayer for peace, create their intentions of health, unify – and strengthen the state of mind they were in, to the state of mind they are in now.

Kinslee has overcome every odd and obstacle, alongside her family, and with her great-aunt Sherry's love and support. Thirty-six weeks and four days old, Kinslee's family is overjoyed to share that Kinslee Larue ("Mighty Mouse" as her family calls this "tiny little warrior") is healthier, happier, and continues to smile; is out of the hospital; and is living her life at home with her twin sister and family," Addison emphasizes; "she has the strength and courage from the support of her family, friends, and community which has been placed into the world for Kinslee; as she receives all of the prayers of health, love, and peace that she deserves."

CREATING A RIPPLE EFFECT
– 47 –

Scott and Marla:

The beautiful vision of the Intention Stick, from pure love and pure intention, is that everyone in the world will be wearing a Tree of Life Intention Stick; and with intentions available in every language, each person will insert the Intention of *Oneness* at the same time. The energy of choosing intentions together is to create this unifying aspect for healing and peace.

If we can connect with one soul, to be a guiding hand in their journey, to uplift and inspire, then the soul has the potential to become a guiding hand for someone else, to uplift and inspire; such is the ripple effect of casting a beautiful pebble.

When we inspire and uplift someone who doesn't feel loved, to feel loved; who doesn't feel that they have meaning in their life, to feel meaning in their life; and someone who may not feel a connection to their purpose, to connect with a purpose; then we inspire and uplift the person to connect with their self, with their family and friends, with their community, and by extension, the world.

This is the ripple effect which we create through the connections we uplift and inspire in self and others, thereby becomes a blessing of light for the world. Like the philosophy and story of Ubuntu – which emphasizes the art of working together as a whole, (rather than the individual working alone, separately, and apart from the whole), we therefore co-operate and co-create with one another: I AM because WE ARE.

WHY AM I HERE?
– 48 –

"Why am I here?" By approaching this question through the lens of affirming "I am" first, is significant; because "I am" affirms oneself within the present moment. Let us contemplate and consider this question from a different lens: "I am here, why?" The consideration of this question, written in this way, helps to encourage, facilitate, and support the conversation with one self, and with others, through a unifying aspect of intention; namely, twenty-two words of intention:

I AM: *Oneness ... Believe ... Faith ... Gratitude ... Be, Let it Be ... Love ... Light ... Blessed ... Peace ... Kindness ... Health ... Consciousness ... Inspire ... Laugh ... Joy ... Courage ... Happiness ... Spiritual ... Trust ... Knowledge ... Success ... Compassion ...*

The Intention Stick encourages, develops, and supports the transition fromward and forward; thus, towards the transformation of presence we aspire to. As we amplify and scale intentional conversations about presence – how to be present with one another – within in a safe and practical way, it will lead to stronger, more meaningful, (in)tentional boundaries, connections, and experiences.

When we connect to positive intention, we arrive with consciousness; when we arrive with this state of awareness, we're conscious of the kinds of decisions that we make. Thus, with this state of being, we create certainty and enthusiasm. Therefore, we attend to where we're going and what we're doing "for the world, with the planet, from the whole."

We believe it is our responsibility to consciously choose to be in a positive state of awareness, this positive state of being; thus, so we can be intentional about our boundaries, connections, and experiences.

Intention Gifts Attention
– 49 –

Intention (such as *love*) is a guiding force that helps heal, and helps build inner peace. As one combines their intention (of *love*) in relation to other intentions (i.e., *peace* and *health*), this improves, focuses, and strengthens upon this guiding force to therefore help further evolve and expand the intention gifts attention approach; that is, within the overall progress, as one moves forward to heal and form inner peace.

The intention (of *love*) in relation to, and combination with two intentions establishes something exceptionally remarkable for an individual to perceive... an entirely new approach, perspective, and outcome. And – as a dynamic balance within – this *creates*: an effect to help heal one self and others; the space and place to demonstrate the intention of presence; an intention gifts attention *experience* for the individual to celebrate with self and/ or with others; and the space and place to *shift* consciousness from negative, to *positive* experience: from past, to *present* experience: from an unaware, to an *aware* experience: from a lost sense of self, to a *found* sense of self. Thus, to shine light.

Connections between individuals that are either based on two people, or based on three or more people, bring their points of view to their own conversations and connections – which cause to shape their relations with one another. From the point of view of intention gifts attention to the peaceful and healing *approach-perspective-outcome*, each person seeks to develop, encourage, and support the common good and presence of one another, within the unifying aspect of oneness.

THE VISION FOR THE TREE OF LIFE MOVEMENT
– 50 –

Dear Scott and Marla,

I am now writing in rather more formal terms to ask if the two of you would please consider an invitation from us to become two of our international Leadership Fellows. I have now discussed this with Father Hueston and am writing on his behalf to say that we would be delighted - and privileged - if you would consider becoming two of our Fellows.

As I said when you were with us, we're still in the early days of establishing the Society. We are very clear about our overall mission of "leaders nurturing each other's wisdom" and have identified a number of key themes - such as leaders going from good to exceptional and leading culture change - that we are already developing with our current group of founding Fellows. We are also clear that we want to co-create our future themes with Fellows, which is why I'm reaching out to a small number of you involved in last week's remarkable experience in the hope that you will want to join us in growing this initiative as a significant movement for change (alongside the Tree of Life movement!).

It goes without saying that we are very aware that there's rather a lot of water and land that separate us (!) and the deal we have with international Fellows is that we only expect to be able to see them when it works out for them. If you were to say yes and could join us once next year, that would be AMAZING - and if it is more like 2018 before we see you again, that would be great, too, and no surprise given how hectic your lives are!

The idea behind this is NOT to put you under any additional pressure. It's simply our way of saying that we think you are two exceptional individuals and we feel very blessed that you came to the House and want to keep the bond there on whatever terms are manageable for you.

For me personally, one of the great attractions of you becoming Leadership Fellows is that it would give the House a special relationship with the two of you. So if there is ever anything that you want to do, and could usefully involve the House, it would be so much easier for us to discuss it because you will already be part of the fellowship - as well as our family that came together again last week after many incarnations apart!!

So, you two, I'm in your hands! If you want to talk on the phone, that would be great, of course. If you're up for going for it and taking stock as we go, then all you need to say is "We're In" and we'll take it from there.

And if this doesn't feel right at the moment, please just say and you know I will completely respect that.

It's great that we know that in one way or another, we will keep alongside each other as we sit in our tents under the Tree of Life, occasionally venturing out for a drink and a few somersaults - delivered rather more elegantly by some than others!

Thanks for everything, you two, with love and all very very best,

Pete xx

ENDING NOTE TO READER

——

An ancient Greek Proverb, which resonates with us, emphasizes: "A society grows great when old men plant trees, the shade of which they know they will never sit in."

From the point of view that intention gifts attention to stay present, the Tree of Life Movement founded, and created, the Tree of Life Intention Stick. In its practical application, this is an intention-based technology, applied by the use of this spiritual tool: which is a constant and physical reminder of your intentions, as one selects, shares, and wears their intentions over their heart; from which encourages all persons to connect with and attend to self, family, friends, and their community – and, by extension, the world – for more meaningful, (in)tentional boundaries, connections, and experiences.

From the perspective of meaningful connections and extraordinary experiences, we arrive through the way in which we think and feel about "being for the world, with the planet, from the whole."

* * *

A Noteworthy Experience

***Celebrate Your
Intention Gifts Attention
Experience!***

Tree of Life Movement Journal

* * *

To gift an Intention Stick, or receive one,
(as a gift for yourself), please visit:
www.intentionstick.org

Our Intention Blessing
For You, Dear Reader

———

C lose your eyes and take a deep breath through your nose so you can ground yourself. First and foremost, may you receive blessings of health and light and love and courage and strength and everything each and every one of you needs in your life right now to continue to fill up your beautiful hearts and souls with unconditional love which will allow you to fully heal. Which will allow you to continue to help so many more brothers and sisters heal. Which will unify all mankind and bring us back together as one so we should all see heaven on earth as it is here now and see your true purpose in life and be your authentic self.

Our Purpose and Mission

———

Our purpose is to shift consciousness and awaken
people to the powers with themselves; to transform
personal circumstances; and to create positive change
in world; ultimately, connecting all humanity as one.

* * *

Our mission is to unify the collective of humanity
through a global spiritual awakening, ignited by
the realization of the power held by intention.

With Gratitude, Light, and Love,
The Tree of Life Movement

* * *

"Changing the world one tree at a time … we become one.™